What Would You Do?

FIRE IN THE NIGHT

By Sandra D. Bricker

Teenage BOOKS

Group
Loveland, Colorado

Credits
Edited by Stephen Parolini
Cover and book designed by Judy Bienick
Cover and illustrations by Peg Magovern

Library of Congress Cataloging-in-Publication Data
Bricker, Sandra D., 1958-
    Fire in the night / by Sandra D. Bricker.
      p.   cm.—(What would you do?)
    Summary: The reader's decisions control seventeen-year-old Donna's search for spiritual truth and meaning. Uses a Christian perspective to explore the issues of occultism, cults, and the New Age movement.
    ISBN 1-55945-047-9
    1. Plot-your-own stories. [1. Occultism—Fiction. 2. Christian life—Fiction. 3. Plot-your-own stories.] I. Title. II. Series.
PZ7.B7593Fi 1991
[Fic]—dc20   91-21929
          CIP
          AC

Printed in the United States of America

Dedication

To my mom, Jess ...
who taught me to weigh all the variables
and make choices I can live with.
And to my "mom in Christ," Tone ...
who taught me to live with
the choices I make.
Growing up and chasing dreams is much easier
when you have a support system to back you up.
I thank the Lord for blessing me with you both!

Your Road Map

Imagine you see a strange cat stretched out in the sun outside your kitchen window. The cat sleepily yawns, half grins at you, blinks its green eyes and wriggles the thick fur up and down its back. The cat looks sweet, cuddly, safe. Do you approach it?

Not all things that look harmless and inviting really are. That cat *might* roll over on its side and expose a soft, furry belly to be stroked; but, just as easily, it could swipe at your hand before you ever get close enough to pet it.

Life's choices hold the same possibilities. The choices we make, even in the simplest situations, can alter our course and change our lives forever. Without careful consideration, we can end up in the middle of circumstances beyond our control, even when our intentions are initially good.

Fire in the Night explores the decisions—great and small—of a 17-year-old named Donna. In her search for spiritual truth and meaning, Donna encounters many obstacles, and the right path to take is not always evident or clear. As with that cat on the window sill, some situations are almost irresistible in their allure. Their outcomes may be just as satisfying—or far more dangerous.

You're invited to take this journey with Donna. Begin on the first page of the story and make the choices as they are made available to you, turning to the specified page to continue the story. Complete a story line to its end, and then go back and read another story line to discover the consequences of different decisions.

It's okay to make wrong decisions in this book—you can learn from them. Just be careful if you face these tough decisions in real life.

Fire in the Night

Donna's stomach dropped to her knees and then catapulted back up past her throat and shakily down into place again. Her own screams sounded muffled, as if they were coming from far off in the distance. She was holding so tight to the bar in front of her she could hardly feel her fingers.

As the roller coaster came rolling to a stop, Donna Farron pulled herself up and stumbled out onto the platform.

"Wanna go again?" her friend, Bob, called out to her above the buzz of excitement.

"Again?" she tried to laugh as she made her way to the exit turnstile. "Enough already! There are other rides at the fair besides this roller coaster!"

Donna wondered why she'd let Bob talk her into that third excursion. Her head was still spinning and her heart still pounding as she made her way down the stairs toward the ground—which seemed to be moving.

"Wait for me!" shouted Bob. "I'm going one more time."

Donna's dark chestnut-color hair danced as she walked unsteadily toward the others from her church youth group. Her brown eyes glimmered in the afternoon sunlight. While most of her girlfriends looked like they could be cheerleaders, Donna had a natural beauty—unassuming and appealing. She was completely unaware of it, of course, and that made her approachable.

"I don't know how he does it," Donna marveled to her companions waiting on the other side of the gate.

"Isn't this his fourth time?" asked Shari.

"This is the best time our youth group has ever had!" Laura said before Donna had a chance to respond.

Donna was having the time of her life, and she was especially happy she was in Kevin's group. She'd been watching him for months but never had the courage to strike up a conversation. She looked at him now with fresh appreciation. His light gold hair and crystal blue eyes were striking.

Donna watched how Kevin talked with the others. He was always the leader, the one in control. Donna wished she had that quality. She was more the quiet one, the follower rather than the planner.

"What're we gonna do next?" asked Kevin.

"Let's wait for Bob," Laura suggested, "then we can head to the booths. We're all supposed to meet up with Tim back there in an hour or so anyway."

By the time Bob staggered down from the platform after his fourth dizzying ride, he was eager to move on to something a little more sedate than The Hurricane. The game booths were just the thing.

Donna, Bob and Kevin made their way to the ring toss while Shari, Laura and Tom took their chances at the shooting gallery. When they came back together again, they found themselves in front of the fortuneteller's tent.

"How about this?" suggested Tom with a glint in his eye. "Fortunes, anyone?"

"No way!" Bob flared. "A fortuneteller?"

"What could it hurt?" asked Laura.

"It's harmless," Kevin assured them as he snatched Donna's arm and led her to the entrance of the tent. "Shall we?" Donna couldn't believe he was asking her.

The light faintly flickered on the other side of the lavender veil hanging from ceiling to ground between Donna and "Rosalee the Seer."

"Come in," she heard someone say in a raspy, cryptic voice. "Don't be afraid. Step through the curtain."

"Go on," Laura said.

Donna could feel her pulse pounding in her temples, but she wasn't sure if it was because of the fortuneteller's mystery or because she was so close to Kevin.

Kevin sang, "Oooh-oooh-oooh," in a half-eerie, half-comedic voice. "Well?"

Donna and Kevin leaned into the entrance of the tent.

What would you do?

If Donna goes inside, turn to page 17.
If she does not go in, turn to page 35.

"Uh, no thanks," Tanya stammered. "Aren't you a Christian?"

"What's that supposed to mean?" Donna challenged.

"Well, I'm a Christian too," Tanya told her. "The Bible says astrology is wrong."

Donna felt her face burning—not out of anger but out of embarrassment. A scripture flashed across her mind. Something about meat. If someone else thinks it's wrong for you to eat it, don't eat it. Don't make others stumble in their faith. It was a verse in I Corinthians. Yes, I Corinthians 8:13.

"Sorry. I didn't mean to offend you," Donna finally said, but Tanya had already whisked away from the table.

Donna was immersed in what Tanya had said. She realized dabbling in horoscopes had directly damaged her relationship with another Christian. She couldn't shake the confusion in Tanya's eyes, the look that said, "What kind of Christian are you?" And Donna wondered the same thing.

"What kind of Christian am I?"

That night during Donna's prayer time, she asked that question again.

"What kind of Christian am I, Lord?" she whispered. "I guess I haven't been serving you the way I know I should. Help me encourage others rather than cause them to falter in their faith. Help me avoid things that point me away from you. Guide me, Lord. Amen."

As she rolled over onto her side in her soft bed, Donna felt confident God would provide answers to her prayers.

And she knew she wouldn't be searching the horoscope section to find them.

The End

"It's not exactly my kind of reading," Donna admitted. "I've looked at stuff like that before, and I've decided I really don't like it. It goes against my beliefs."

"Looking out for yourself is against your principles?" Karen asked.

"No. But Jesus taught us we should love everyone. And I just don't like what this book says about gratification—it sounds selfish and foolish."

"I feel sorry for you," Karen said. "I think you're fooling yourself."

"I'm not," Donna said with a hint of a smile. "But thanks for your concern."

■

The next afternoon, Donna stood at her locker, blankly staring at the books she had to choose from for her next class. But she was thinking more about Karen than chemistry class.

"Amnesia,?" she heard someone say, and Donna turned to find her neighbor, Susan, standing a few feet away.

"Huh?"

"Amnesia," Susan repeated. "Can't remember what classes you're in?"

"Oh, yeah," Donna laughed. "I guess I have more important things on my mind than classes and homework."

"Don't we all," Susan smiled as she breezed through the combination on her own locker a few yards down.

"You're a Christian, aren't you?" Donna asked, certain that Susan was.

"Yes," she replied curiously. "Why?"

"One of my friends," Donna began, not even sure why she was telling Susan, "is into all that occult and New Age stuff. And I was talking to her yesterday ... I'm not sure how to tell her what I believe."

Susan nodded knowingly. "That *is* a tough one. But, you know, my pastor has taught on the New Age movement a couple of times. My church is real good at helping people who are mixed up like that. Maybe you'd like to come to church with me? Pastor Wyman might be able to help."

Donna hadn't thought of going anywhere with Susan in almost seven years. They'd been friends once, but their relationship fizzled out about the same time they lost interest in Barbie dolls, and Donna wondered what it would be like at Susan's church.

"That might be nice," she said finally.

"Great! I'll call you!"

Donna watched Susan as she headed off down the corridor. "Hey! You walking home now?"

"Yes," Susan answered. "Wanna walk along?"

The two old friends headed out the door and down the school steps toward home, already laughing and talking as if they'd been together all the time.

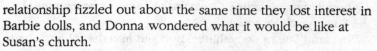

Sunday morning came quickly. Donna was excited about visiting Susan's church and talked comfortably with Susan and her family on the way to church.

Blind choice:

Without looking ahead, turn to page 55 or page 64 to see what kind of church Susan attends.

"Where have you been?" Donna asked Bob as he sauntered into the Sunday school room.

"Why, am I late or something?" Bob slid into the folding chair next to Donna. "What's up?"

"You wouldn't believe it," she replied.

"Try me."

"My parents are getting a divorce," stated Donna.

"Are you kidding?" he asked. "Well, I guess you wouldn't be kidding."

"My dad just blurted it right out," she told him. "Hi, honey, I'm home. Where's the paper? Any coffee made? I want a divorce."

"Donna, I'm really sorry," Bob comforted.

"What's happening to my family, Bob?" And before she knew it, she was in tears. One minute she was composed, and the next she was a mess. She hated her emotions, and she hated their unpredictability. "I can't figure out why this happened," she went on. "I wonder all the time if I had something to do with it."

"Donna, you know you didn't," he assured her. "How could you?"

"He didn't even stick around long enough to face me," she said. "I have all this stuff built up inside me, things I'd like to say to him, names I'd like to call him for leaving us without any warning."

"You wanna ditch Sunday school today?" Bob suggested. "We could go get some doughnuts and talk awhile."

"Yeah," Donna nodded, dabbing her eyes with a tissue.

Donna and Bob left Sunday school behind them and headed over to Bob's. They talked for more than an hour. But Donna was still upset. Later that night, Donna looked at the stack of videos and paperback books Bob had loaned her.

She randomly chose one of the tapes and poked it into the VCR. As she was waiting for the tape to play, she noticed her father smiling at her from one of the photos on the mantle. She turned the photo face down before sinking back in front of the television.

A balding man with an annoying, scratchy little voice appeared, midword. Bob had forgotten to rewind the tape.

"If you don't care about yourself," the man crackled, "no one else will either."

Donna pushed the rewind button, picked up one of the

books and skimmed through it while the video rewound.

"The most common thing for the child to do," she read from page 26 of the book in her hand, "is to blame himself for the breakup of the marriage. This is a dangerous situation. It can actually be life-threatening. The following techniques are useful in helping the child deal with the reality of the divorce."

The tape clicked to a stop as it reached the beginning, but Donna ignored it, opting to settle back and sink into the book. She read the chapter titles: "Role-Playing"; "Visualization: Creating a More Peaceful Place"; "Positive Thinking Exercises"; and "Positive Reinforcement of Divorce."

The last one seemed odd to Donna, and she scanned quickly over the text. The author was suggesting, if the divorce is an unalterable reality, the parents should try making it seem more appealing to the child to have two separate parents and households rather than one single family unit.

"What're you reading?" Donna's mom asked as she walked in the front door.

"Something Bob gave me on coping with divorce," Donna replied, her eyes still glued to the book.

"What do you think of it? Is it any good?" her mom asked.

What would you do?

If Donna decides the material is good, turn to page 61.
If she decides it's not very good, turn to page 57.

Kurt's arguments on the benefits of D&D hardly seemed to matter when Donna read about Alan Kirkland's suicide the next morning on page 6 of the Tribune.

Alan's 6-year-old sister found him on the floor of his bedroom, wrists slashed and blood everywhere—still clad in his macabre Halloween costume. Donna discovered later he'd pinned a note to his cape. It simply read: "Just another in a long line of humiliations—finally, the end."

Donna recalled the look she'd seen in Alan's eyes the night before, as his character had been pressed against the wall and his enemy's sword to his throat.

Donna knew all about the humiliation that drove Alan to such a drastic end. Karen and Kurt would never admit it, but Donna knew. In her heart, she knew. The warning had been right there in Alan's eyes the night before, but no one, not even Donna, had been able to decipher it.

Donna met Susan on the way to school the next Monday morning. She'd known Susan since they were both very young, but they'd drifted apart early on. Donna didn't know why, but she explained the whole creepy story to Susan in just a few minutes.

"I know Alan," Susan commented when she heard the news. "I mean, I knew him. He took me to the freshman dance."

It was hard for Donna to imagine Susan ever having had a date with Alan Kirkland. Susan seemed so plain to Donna.

"You know," Susan finally said, "my pastor has taught on the occult several times. Maybe you'd like to come to church with me on Sunday?"

"Oh, I don't know."

"Come on," Susan pushed. "It'd be fun. You and I haven't done anything together in such a long time."

It was unsettling to Donna that Susan remembered how close they'd once been.

"Yeah, okay," Donna tried to smile. "It might be fun."

And Donna found herself looking more and more forward to it as each day passed that week. Visiting Susan's church would be fun. The prospect took her mind off what had happened to Alan. Donna was grateful for that.

Blind choice:
Without looking ahead, turn to page 55 or page 64.

"Are you changing religions on me?" Mom asked.

"No, Mom," answered Donna. "I'm just curious about this kind of stuff. I didn't want to scare you by leaving this out for you to see."

"I believe you, Donna. But I wish you wouldn't hide stuff from me."

"Oh, I won't, Mom. I'm sorry."

"Well ... that's okay. We've both been under a lot of stress lately. Just don't let your curiosity about that stuff become an obsession. If you have any questions, talk to me."

"Thanks, Mom."

Mom turned and headed into the kitchen.

Donna wondered for a moment why her mom hadn't been upset about the book. Perhaps she was still preoccupied with the divorce.

The divorce! I was hoping I wouldn't have to deal with that again, thought Donna. She slumped down onto her bed.

Donna thought about looking at the book that night, looking for anything that might help her deal with her pain. But the book didn't hold the same interest it had before. What she needed was someone to talk to. Yet she felt suddenly drained. Too tired to talk. Too worn out to think.

Maybe she'd talk to Karen at school on Monday. Or maybe she'd confide in Bob.

What would you do?

If she talks to Bob, turn to page 10.
If she talks to Karen, turn to page 51.

But after a while, Donna grew tired of the group and all their strange goings-on. Her grades had slipped dramatically because of all the late nights. Her fascination with drawing blood for Satan waned after doing it so many times, and she began to participate less and less.

Eventually, the day came when Donna realized she was a Satanist in name only; she was no longer practicing what was once her religion. She looked at herself in the mirror and noticed her skin was white and her eyes just limp pools of black and white.

"Who am I?" she wondered aloud as she stared at her own reflection.

Donna didn't feel much purpose in life anymore and could hardly remember a time when she had. Even as a member of the coven, she'd only lived for the moment—for the parties and the drugs and the excitement.

"Maybe that's how life is," she deduced. "Maybe there's just nothing much to it. What's the use of even living?"

Donna reached for a bottle of pills ...

The End

Donna had never seen that look in Chaz's eyes.

"Rhonda," she cried, turning away from Chaz. "Rhonda, please. Help me reason with them."

"However long life is," Rhonda snickered coldly, "that's how long you're in."

"Forget it!" Donna shouted. "I'm out!" And she darted toward the door.

Before she knew it, hands grabbed Donna from all directions. Someone pulled her by the hair and slammed her to the floor. Donna tried to scream, but someone stuffed something in her mouth so she couldn't make a sound.

Things happened so fast. Someone ripped at her clothes, tearing into her skin with the zipper of her own jeans. Then Chaz fell on top of her with a thud.

"You'll never get out," he promised her. "There's no getting out."

Pain and fear gripped Donna as Chaz brutally raped her. Someone cut into her bare stomach with a knife and engraved something there.

"You're branded now," the one she had known only as Merlin cackled. "In life or in death, you'll still be Satan's child!"

Blood spilled from her body as she dug her fingers deep into the carpet beneath her. Someone yanked the gag from her mouth, but she nearly choked as someone forced pill after pill down her throat and poured water down her mouth and nose.

Donna knew Chaz and the others were carrying her somewhere, but the drugs had already begun to take their dulling effect. She couldn't think clearly about what was happening. The hum of the moving car and the whoosh of fresh night air rushing through an open window gave her a momentary deliverance from the pandemonium taking place around her.

"Dear Jesus!" she called out in her mind. "Help me! Help me!"

The last thing Donna heard was laughter before she felt her body fly through the air. The car must have been going 60 miles an hour when they hurled her naked body out the open door.

◼

"It's a miracle she wasn't killed," the doctor said over Donna from the side of her bed. "A miracle, pure and simple. It's as if her body was thrown from that car packed in insulation. Her injuries are minor in comparison with what should've happened in those circumstances."

"Our God is a God of miracles," Donna heard her mother sniff. "And I'll never stop thanking him for sparing my Donna."

Three or four images of Donna's mother blended into one as Donna opened her sore eyes.

"Honey?" said Mom excitedly.

Donna smiled up at her mother standing over her. She'd never been so happy to see anyone. "Hi," she managed.

"That's the most beautiful word I think I've ever heard out of you," Mom beamed. "How do you feel?"

"Glad to be alive," she whimpered. "Glad to be alive."

"Thank God," her mom added.

"The coven . . ."

"Everything's going to be all right," her mom interrupted. "It's all over. You're going to be fine."

Donna sighed. A new lifeline to hang on to. Everything was going to be fine.

"You're going to be just fine," Mom repeated, and Donna believed her with all her heart.

The coven behind her, Donna pledged to start a new life. And she vowed to be much more careful with it this time, of that she was certain.

"Thank you, Lord," her mom whispered. "Thank you, Lord!"

Donna forced a smile from her bruised and broken mouth. She knew the coven might still come after her. But she also knew God would be with her. Yes, thank you, Lord, she thought peacefully.

The End

Donna wanted to take someone's hand as she entered Rosalee's tent, but she knew the others would tease her unmercifully if she did. So she took a deep breath, tossed the veil aside and stepped through. The flickering candles sent shadows dancing across the tent walls, and the smoky smell of incense burned Donna's nostrils. The rest of the group entered behind her. Donna noticed Bob hadn't come in with them.

"You're seeking answers to many questions," Rosalee half sneered at them. "Tell me, what would you like to know first?"

Donna giggled, partly out of amusement but mostly out of nervousness. "I don't know," she finally said.

"You tell us," Kevin said boldly. "You're the one with the crystal ball."

"All right," Rosalee glared. "I shall begin with this one." Donna felt Rosalee's eyes pierce through her. "Your name, please?"

"D-Donna."

"Donna," Rosalee repeated, and it sounded different when she said it in her Russian-Italian-maybe Greek accent. "You are much the romantic one."

Her friends snickered.

"You seek romance, danger, adventure. But you are never quite satisfied. Life is never quite exciting enough for you."

Donna wanted to nod in agreement, and in fact she would've if her friends hadn't been there. She was always dreaming. Always living vicariously through the characters in books and movies. Always tuning in to see what the sophisticated heroines of Hollywood were up to next.

"You have had much happiness in your young life, though," Rosalee went on. "You are known as joyful, optimistic. I'm sorry this will change for a little while, though. Something very sad will happen soon, something unexpected and sad."

"What about me?" Tom chimed in. Donna wanted to smack him and tell him to shut up and let Rosalee continue. She didn't though. Instead, she faked a look of disbelief and sat in her chair.

Donna didn't hear the rest of Rosalee's predictions. She was lost in her own thoughts about what terrible thing might happen to make her sad. She wondered if she really would face such a dramatic event. What if it really was true! What if ...

∎

Rosalee the Seer was all but forgotten when Donna came racing through the front door early that evening. She could hardly wait to tell her mom about her day, about The Hurricane and about being in Kevin's group.

"Mom? Dad?" she called, tossing her jacket carelessly across the back of the chair. "Anybody home?"

The house was mostly dark, except for the light trickling out from beneath her parents' bedroom door. She started past it, heading for her own room. Then she noticed something wasn't right. She could hear someone crying.

"Mom?"

"Yes, Donna," Mom sniffed. "Come in."

Donna opened the door and entered to find her mother sitting on the edge of the bed, her face red and careworn.

"Mom, what is it?" Donna asked as she sat down. "What's happened? Is it Daddy?"

"Yes," Mom whispered. "But it's not what you think."

"Is he okay?"

"Yes," she tried to laugh. "Just great."

"Mom!" Donna scolded. "Come on. Tell me what's going on!"

"He's left me," Mom said through serious, tear-filled eyes. "He's left us."

"What?" Donna couldn't think. It wasn't sinking in. It wasn't making sense. Her father would never ...

"He wants a divorce," Mom told her carefully. "He doesn't want to be married anymore. I don't know if there's someone else ... he said there wasn't ... but he's gone."

Donna barely heard the rest. She felt like she was slipping away, into shock maybe. Sadness began to grip at her with catlike claws. How could this be happening?

It suddenly hit her, like a cold, wet blanket dropped from nowhere: Rosalee's prediction! Donna's eyes welled with tears. Was it just a coincidence? Or did Rosalee really have the power to foresee this horrible event in Donna's private life?

What would you do?

If Donna decides the fortuneteller knew about the divorce, turn to page 39.

If she thinks it's just a coincidence, turn to page 42.

Loving her mom and going back to the life she ran away from were two entirely different things. Donna couldn't go home now. She just couldn't. No one understood, she concluded. No one. Why couldn't they just understand she'd found something really good?

The letter from her mom inspired Donna to work harder to make her new life work. She became involved in every aspect of the community, and she was especially fervent in her servanthood to Pastor Wyman, her spiritual leader, and to Susan's father, his closest assistant.

■

It was quite ironic when Pastor Wyman, who viewed illness as evidence of weak faith, contracted pneumonia. A cold he'd refused to acknowledge or treat had escalated so quickly no one could've anticipated its outcome. Six days short of Donna's third year at the promised land known as Evergreen Community, Pastor Wyman died.

Weeks passed filled with mourning and confusion. Finally a group meeting conducted by Susan's father, Arnold, was held, and he announced his plans to take over for their late leader.

To some, this seemed the natural succession, since Arnold had been Pastor Wyman's closest assistant. To others, though, no one but Pastor Wyman could or should lead them. Over half the members of their community packed up and left for various destinations.

Donna decided to remain out of loyalty to Susan's family, and she worked hard to serve Arnold the way she had served Pastor Wyman. But Donna didn't find that same spark in Arnold, that same fire, and it began to discourage her.

But what else could she do? There was no one else to follow.

The End

A few weeks later, Donna and several other kids her age were soliciting donations outside an Arizona shopping mall—not far from the "promised land" Pastor Wyman had led them to. She was happy to be supporting her church's work—and Pastor Wyman's vision for building a huge chapel on the hill overlooking the barracklike building that had become her new home.

"Would you like to buy a flower?" Donna was the first to approach a passer-by. "The money supports our church."

"No!" was the quick response. No one wanted to listen to what she had to say.

Donna looked up just in time to see a van screeching into a U-turn at the intersection. She stood there frozen as it screamed to a stop right next to where she was standing. A man jumped from the van and grabbed Donna's arm. Amid her screams and squeals, he tossed her inside the van, locked the door, quickly climbed inside and raced the van away from the mall before Donna could understand what was happening to her.

"Donna!" she heard Susan scream after the van.

"Donna, you're safe now," said a voice from inside the van. Donna looked up at the source of the comforting voice.

Her mother looked back at her.

"You won't get away with this," Donna screamed. "I'll just run back home, back to my church!"

"That church is not your home," her mom began. "You've been brainwashed, Donna. Your home is with us."

"Not anymore!"

And so it went for hours.

Joe Dial was an expert in deprogramming cult members, and he had devised a plan to take Donna somewhere private for as long as it took to deprogram her.

After hours of travel, the van made a quick stop for provisions and then headed to a secluded campground. The van was loaded with tents, sleeping bags and a huge Coleman stove. It angered Donna even more to know her kidnapping had been planned to such detail.

Not responding to them, she decided, would be her best defense, and she resolved not to speak no matter what they said. And as soon as they weren't looking, as soon as she could manage it, she would escape and get back to Pastor Wyman and her new family.

For three days, they talked to her. They pushed their ideas on her, their concepts for her life, but Donna didn't budge. Not a word came out of her. Once, when she thought she saw her chance, she bolted from the campground, but Joe tackled her. He carried her back, kicking and screaming, and zipped her in the tent until she calmed down.

"What's it going to take to get through to you, Donna?" her mom sobbed that night from the other side of the campfire. "Why can't you see how much you're loved ... "

She couldn't finish because of the tears. Donna watched as her mother began to sob uncontrollably. Joe moved in and put his arm around her shoulder, but she didn't even seem to notice.

"God, forgive me," she finally managed to get out. "If I could've given Donna a stable home—if she would've been loved the way she needed to be. If ... " She almost choked on the word "if."

Donna had never seen her mother this upset.

Blind choice:

Without looking ahead, turn to page 41 or page 103.

Donna's face grew red with embarrassment. She wasn't embarrassed at having the book; she was embarrassed at getting caught trying to hide it.

"It's just a book."

Her mother paused for several moments. "You know how I feel about that kind of thing, Donna."

"Mom ... "

"Pick it up and follow me."

"But, Mom!" Donna protested. "Mom!"

"Follow me!" her mom ordered.

Donna reluctantly did as she was told. "Mom, I'm not a child," she snapped as she followed down the hallway. "It's just a book I wanted to read. It's ... "

"In there," Mom interrupted, pointing to the fireplace. "Toss it in."

"Come on," Donna pleaded, and then her voice suddenly turned to a shriek. "This isn't fair!"

"In the fireplace," Mom insisted.

Donna finally let the book slip from her hands into the fireplace. When she looked at her mother, she noticed the anger that smoldered in her mom's eyes now looked strangely like worry.

"I won't have this kind of trash in my home, Donna," she sighed. "You know that."

"You are so out of touch! Don't you think you're going a little overboard here?"

"Light it, Donna." She handed Donna a book of matches. Donna looked hard into her mother's pale face, and then hesitantly lit a match and tossed it down onto the book. When the match fizzled without igniting the book, Donna's mom grabbed the book of matches and carefully lit the book aflame.

As Donna's new-found book of wisdom went up in flames, she turned and headed out of the living room.

"Hold it right there," called her mother. Donna stopped where she was without turning to look back. "This incident is not going unpunished."

"You've already made me burn my book," Donna yelled. "What else would you like? Am I grounded? Fine."

"You are not to come within 20 yards of material like this from now on. And for the next two weeks, you will read five chapters of the Bible every day. Any questions?"

Donna didn't answer. After a few moments of piercing silence, she half whispered, "Can I go now?"

"To your room."

"Where else?" Donna groaned as she rounded the corner and ran to her room.

■

"Five chapters a day!" Karen echoed at Donna when she heard the news the next day at Karen's house.

"Last night it was King Hezekiah," Donna grimaced. "Tonight it will probably be someone else I've never heard of."

"Try reading five chapters a day of *this* bible!" said Karen. She produced a book from beneath her bed and slid it across the comforter toward Donna.

The Satanic Bible.

Donna gasped. Mom would explode if she caught me reading that book, she thought. Maybe I should read it just to get even.

But Donna had begun to wonder if her mom may have been right about playing around with the occult. The book *Mystical Practices had* made her feel a little uncomfortable.

"Open it up. Read a little," Karen urged. "It's pretty interesting."

Slowly, cautiously, Donna opened the book and began to randomly read from it. "Satan represents indulgence, instead of abstinence ... Satan represents kindness to those who deserve it, instead of love wasted on ingrates ... Satan represents all of the so-called sins, as they all lead to physical, mental or emotional gratification ... "

After a few moments, Karen leaned in close to Donna. "What do you think?"

What would you do?

If she gets engrossed by what she reads, turn to page 30.
If she gets turned off, turn to page 8.

"I really like all the people here, and I'm so glad we've gotten close again," Donna began, "but I just don't feel like this is where I'm supposed to be. I have too many questions, I see too many things I don't quite understand or agree with."

"Like what?" Susan asked.

"It's nothing against you or your church, Susan," Donna tried to explain. "I just don't see enough of Jesus here. I see worship, but not of Jesus. Just worship of Pastor Wyman."

Susan didn't respond. Her smile turned into a look of disgust, and she just walked away.

The following Friday Donna met her friends from church at Zebo's Pizza and told them all about the retreat experience.

"I was treated like some sort of alien the whole next day," she told them. "I did learn something important though. If we don't give people the love and acceptance they crave when they come to our church, they'll just go out looking for it somewhere else. And 'somewhere else' could be dangerous."

The others nodded and continued to munch away at their pizza. Donna was glad to be back among her friends.

Then Donna noticed Melanie—a girl who wasn't too popular at school—walking into the restaurant with her younger brother, Thad.

"Melanie!" she called out and hurried toward her. "Are you here to eat?"

"Yes," the girl said timidly. "My mom's in the hospital and Dad's not much of a cook, so it's pizza again."

"You wanna join us? We have more than enough."

Melanie's face lit up.

"You got any mushroom?" Thad asked.

"Not yet," Donna said as she led them to the table, "but the way this group eats we'll have to order more anyway."

Thad and Melanie followed her over to the table surrounded by her friends from church.

"This is a friend of mine from school—Melanie. And her brother, Thad," she announced. "They're going to join us."

Donna smiled as she saw how warmly the group accepted Melanie. Why had I ever wanted to look elsewhere for acceptance? Donna wondered.

As she sat down, Donna prayed a silent little prayer.

Dear God, help me demonstrate in my own life the same powerful love and acceptance I thought I'd found at Susan's church. But teach me to focus on you to find that love. Use me to show others how much you love them.

And help me begin with Melanie.

Amen.

The End

"You know what I think?" Grant spoke up from his place at the back. "I think whatever feels good, do it. You know? Do what's right for you, follow your instincts. Some people like to lean on God for every little thing. *I* think that's a pretty weak way to live—but it's fine for them."

"Grant!" Marla reprimanded. "God wants us to lean on him for everything. That's what he calls us to do, to totally depend on him."

"See, Tim!" Grant half laughed. "This is why I don't speak up more in class."

"I've used meditation techniques before," added Rico. "When I'm real wound up, like if we have problems at home and I want to just get myself back on track. It's helpful."

"Yeah," said Shane. "Jesus promised peace that can be found a lot of different ways."

"Meditating on Jesus is different from just meditating though," insisted Marla. "Meditating and visualization and all that, that's not Christian."

"People say being a vegetarian is New Age," said Grant. "But don't you think God wants us to eat right and take care of our bodies?"

Donna listened intently as the conversation bounced back and forth. Before they knew it, Sunday school was over.

Donna and Bob walked over to the sanctuary together, and all the kids who passed them were still deep in the conversation that had started in Sunday school.

"I've heard about this seminar they're having over at the college," Bob suggested. "It's called Training for Inner Peace. We could pick up some new techniques, learn a little more about how to relax. What d'ya say?"

"When is it?" Donna asked.

"Next weekend. You wanna go?"

"Sure," she answered.

Donna felt good she and Bob were in such total agreement. Peace and harmony. That's the message Jesus preached.

As it turned out, one of Donna's newest friends from school, Tanya Williams, was planning to attend the training seminar with her family. Donna rode with them to the seminar.

Donna embraced the teachings at the seminar and happily agreed to attend a support group with the Williams family.

During the coming days Donna learned about channeling. She was excited to learn she could choose her own spirit guide. This spirit guide would help her through the period of her life she learned was called the awakening. Donna chose Jesus.

■

In the first session with the support group, the class members were told to create a "safe room" in their minds. This would be the place where they could go when things got difficult or tense, and it could look however they wanted it to look. Donna re-created her grandmother's parlor, with its wine-color velvet easy chair, an old and tarnished floor lamp, and fading floral paper on the wall. She had always felt so safe there, and she could almost smell her grandfather's cigar smoke rooted deep in the fabric of the chair.

It was in that room the very next day Donna saw the spirit guide she believed to be Jesus. He entered the room and approached her where she was seated safely in her grandfather's easy chair. When her spirit guide appeared to her, he extended his hand toward her and she took it. Together they floated over a deep green meadow and across a silent ocean into the clouds and back down again.

When the instructor's voice told the class to return to the safe room, then back to a more conscious level, Donna felt sad. I don't want to leave, she thought. I want to stay here where I feel strong—and peaceful. I feel safe here.

Donna began meditating at home in her room, and she often called upon her spirit guide to talk with her and help her make important decisions. Tanya's mother became Donna's mentor, often leading and guiding her into deeper and more peaceful states.

One night, as they were making dinner, Donna's mom asked, "What's the name of the Williamses' church?"

"The name?"

"Yes, Donna," Mom smiled as she sliced a bunch of carrots, "the name. I'm sure it has a name."

"Well, not exactly."

Mom set down the knife and turned full attention to Donna. "What does that mean?"

"Well, it's not exactly a traditional church," Donna admitted. "Not like Pastor Hanley's church."

"You know," her mom began, "I heard you in your room last

night making some low sound in your throat. When I walked in, I stood there for five minutes. You didn't even know I was there, Donna. What's going on? What kind of church is this?"

What would you do?

If Donna gets angry and defensive, turn to page 32.
If she is open and honest, turn to page 68.

"I'm not sure what I think," Donna told her honestly.

"You want to see more?" Karen invited.

"Well ... yes."

"There's a bookstore downtown. It's called Six-Six-Six."

■

Donna might not have noticed the sign if she hadn't looked up to see a bird flutter into the nest it had built in the rafters next door. The sign read "Six-Six-Six." The occult bookstore Karen talked about was right in front of her. She'd landed upon it by accident in the alley behind her mom's favorite antique store and around the corner from the pharmacy.

Donna walked casually up to the blackened window and tried to look in. She couldn't see much from outside, and she started to walk away, then thought again and stepped inside.

Donna went up one aisle and down the other, stopping at the front counter to look at the jewelry display.

"My name is Chaz. Can I help you?" the guy behind the counter asked.

"No," she said. "I'm just looking."

"For anything in particular?"

"I don't know," she admitted. Then noticing an interesting ring in the case, she added, "That's cool."

"Want to try it on?"

Donna nodded. Taking the ring carefully, she slipped it on the index finger of her left hand. The carved serpent wrapped perfectly around her finger and climbed up toward her middle knuckle, and Donna liked the way it looked.

"How much?"

"Eight dollars," he answered.

"Yeah, I'll take it," she smiled.

"Anything else I can help you with?"

Chaz was so friendly it felt natural to Donna to confide in him. "I've never been in one of these kinds of stores before."

"No? Let me show you around."

"Yeah, okay."

Chaz escorted Donna through the aisles, pointing out sections of interest. She didn't buy anything that day except the ring, but Donna felt welcome at Six-Six-Six, comfortable. The place was inviting. And so was Chaz.

Over the next few weeks, Donna went into Six-Six-Six several times. To browse, to read, to talk with Chaz. She hadn't really bought much—just a book on astral travel and another on casting spells—but Chaz always greeted her warmly and talked with her for as long as she felt like hanging around.

The jewelry case was especially inviting to Donna, and one item in particular drew her attention. It was a rhinestone cross on a sparkling gold chain that cost $45, a bit out of Donna's price range.

"I'm surprised to see a cross for sale in here," she told Chaz.

"Look closer," he motioned. "It's an upside-down cross."

Sure enough, it was upside down. "H'm," she sighed. "It sure is pretty."

"You've been looking at that ever since you came in here," Chaz noticed. "Here."

Chaz glanced around the store before pulling the cross out of the case and slipping it into Donna's hand.

"What're you doing?" she said in surprise.

"Take it," he urged. "I'll cover it."

"What? Why?"

"It's a gift. Take it."

What a wonderful gift. She took the cross and tucked it into her pocket.

"Chaz, thanks," she said earnestly.

"You can wear it tonight," he smiled. "We're having a little meeting at my house, and I'd like you to come."

"A meeting?" she wondered.

"A séance," he said softly. "10 o'clock."

What would you do?

If she goes to the séance, turn to page 97.
If she doesn't go, turn to page 52.

"Mom ..."

"What kind of church are the Williamses taking you to anyway?" her mom asked.

"Mom, I've found peace for the first time in my life."

"Is this what I've taught you? to find peace within yourself?" her mom asked.

"You've taught me to be my own person!" Donna half cried. "You taught me to make my own decisions and to be the best person I can be. Why can't you just accept maybe I'm not meant to be your clone? Maybe I'm different from you. I've never been closer to Jesus than I am today. That should make you happy. Instead all you want to do is control how it happens!"

Donna's mom winced but didn't try to stop Donna as she rushed from the room.

■

For several days after their confrontation, Donna and her mother avoided each other quite effectively. Silence became a very noisy companion. It was accompanied by voices of torment, voices that drove a wedge between the two of them and voices that kept both Donna and her mother hurt and angry.

Over the weeks, their periodic stabs at conversation became less and less successful. Everything Donna said jabbed at her mother's heart.

"Where are you going?"

"To Tanya's," Donna would say, and that same old look would form on her mother's face.

"Will you be home for dinner?"

"I dunno. Maybe. Maybe not."

The wedge between them had become unbearable. At the prodding of Tanya and Donna, Mr. and Mrs. Williams finally agreed to let Donna stay with them for a while.

Donna's mom fought the idea at first, but when Donna came home early from school one day armed with weapons of anger, resentment and determination, her tired mom finally gave in.

"I can't live like this, Donna," she conceded. "If it's what you want, go ahead."

■

Donna thought all her problems were solved when she moved the last of her things into Tanya's bedroom. She was happy to share a home with a group of like-minded people. And she was excited about the future.

But Donna discovered she couldn't sleep at night. Something was nagging at her; something had stolen her peace. Week after week, month after month. Something wasn't right, but Donna just couldn't figure out what it was.

Then she remembered a fragment of something Pastor Hanley had said in a sermon. Something about peace in Jesus. She tried to dismiss it and to let go of the Christian cliché—but couldn't.

Donna grew more tired and less focused at school and at her new home. Her life seemed to be an endless parade of days and nights without meaning or importance. Meditation hadn't worked. Yoga hadn't worked. Visualization hadn't worked.

There must be *something* for me, she thought. There must be something that can bring me the inner peace I so desperately want.

And, with that, she drifted off into another night of fitful sleep. The same kind of restless sleep she would have the rest of her life.

The End

The first meeting was poorly attended. But Donna felt encouraged by the participation and enthusiasm of the six people who did show up.

By the third meeting, the attendance had tripled. The discussion of the night focused on the responsibilities of God's people to care for the planet he'd given them.

"He's the creator," Dane said seriously. "We're the caretakers."

After a productive and enjoyable meeting, one of the kids came up to talk with Donna.

"I've really enjoyed this meeting," he began. "And I'd like to know more about your faith. You guys seem really serious about this Christianity thing. I guess I'd like to know more about what it could do for me."

Donna smiled. At that moment she realized all her efforts in starting the outreach group were worthwhile.

She also knew she wasn't alone in her efforts. Dane and Bob had been there with her.

And God was leading the way.

The End

Donna suddenly began to think clearly. She didn't want anything to do with the fortuneteller. Donna turned and walked out of the tent.

"What's the matter?" Kevin teased. "Scared?"

"Not scared," Donna responded. "Just smart. That kind of thing is a waste of time and money. It's a hoax, and it goes against everything we've been taught."

"Well, I'm going in," Kevin retorted. "Anybody else coming?"

Laura and Shari looked at Donna.

"Come on, Donna," Shari encouraged. "It's just for fun."

"There's nothing fun about it," blurted Bob. "And there's nothing *Christian* about it either."

"Come on, Bob," Laura snickered. "The devil doesn't hang out at the fair!"

The others laughed.

"It's no different from the haunted house or The Hurricane," Shari encouraged.

The two girls followed Kevin and Tom inside.

Donna looked at Bob.

"We tried, Donna," Bob said thoughtfully. "We can't make decisions for them. Just for us. And we made the right one. Getting involved in that stuff is dangerous."

Donna remembered those words on the drive home.

When Donna stepped inside the front door of her house, a chill swept over her. She attributed it to coming out of the night air and closed the door behind her.

"Mom? Dad?" she called as she headed into the kitchen. "Mom?"

Donna's mom was slouched in a kitchen chair, a half-empty cup of coffee in front of her. Her face was careworn and red, and tears rolled down her cheeks.

"Mom, what is it?" Donna walked over to her mother.

"It's your father," Mom managed.

"Daddy?" A thousand thoughts ran through Donna's mind all at once. Accidents, injuries, perhaps a heart attack. "What is it? Where is he?"

"He's gone," she said.

"What? What do you mean he's gone? What's happened?"

"He's gone," Mom repeated. "He came home and told me he was leaving. He wants a divorce. And now he's . . . he's gone."

Donna thought her heart had stopped for a moment. Then she realized it wasn't just her heart, it was her whole world. Her father was gone!

Mom was in no shape to talk about it, and Donna was in no shape to hear. How could God let this happen? What would happen to them now?

That night Donna spent a long time looking around her bedroom. It was somewhat childish still, the frilly white comforter atop the ruffled bed skirt. Four different stuffed animals rested on the lace pillows, and several more were placed on the bookshelf and in the corner rocker.

In contrast to the frilly room, Donna's insides were on fire. She was overwhelmed with the need to talk to someone—anyone—about what had happened. She thought first of confiding in Bob; he was such an understanding listener.

Or perhaps Karen, thought Donna. Karen was always so giving, so willing to listen or help. Donna smiled at the thought of Karen, and she was glad the two had become so much closer over the last few months.

Maybe she'd talk to Bob at church. Or perhaps she'd visit Karen.

What would you do?

If she decides to talk to Bob, turn to page 10.
If she decides to talk to Karen, turn to page 51.

The idea of an actual plot seemed overblown to Donna. No matter how well Leland Craine presented his opinions, Donna knew the New Age movement wasn't nearly as diabolical and or- ganized as he said it was. In fact, most of the New Agers Donna had ever known were on the flaky side and had a hard time keeping their own lives organized, much less a whole interna- tional plot against the church.

"This is absurd," she whispered to Bob. "Are you buying any of this?"

Bob made a face at Donna, mimicking the speaker, which let her know he was as turned off as she was.

■

What a waste of a Saturday! The only thing that would make up for it was a trip down to Izzy's for a burger and curly fries! Tim dropped them off at Izzy's on the way home.

"I didn't know what to say to Tim afterward," Donna told Bob as they found their usual booth next to the plants in the window. "I can see that we should be careful, but that was ridiculous. Do you think Tim and his wife really feel the way the speaker does?"

"I don't know." Bob shook his head. "I didn't want to hurt their feelings or anything, but that guy Craine was pretty extreme."

"A demon around every corner," Donna whispered. "Don't order the burger. They're using it in satanic warfare these days, you know."

"And the chocolate shakes," Bob countered. "They're laced with anti-Christian drugs!"

They laughed just as the waitress approached the table.

"Two burgers and two curly fries," Donna ordered, and then added with a grin at Bob, "And two chocolate shakes!"

■

Donna decided to go into town with her friend Karen after school Monday despite the English test she had to study for. They poked around in the usual stores—Walgreen's and the office sup- ply store where Donna often doodled with the different-color pens. Then they made their way to the bookstore on Brand Avenue. Karen headed over to the New Age section.

Donna was reading the back cover of a mystery novel that had just come out when Karen called out to her. "Look at this!"

Donna set the mystery book back on the shelf and rounded the corner to see what Karen had found.

"Wouldn't that guy love to have a copy of this?"

Donna saw Karen was holding a paperback copy of *The Satanic Bible*, and she realized the "guy" Karen was referring to must be Leland Craine. Donna had told Karen the whole story that day.

"Now there's a thoughtful gift for the old guy!" Donna giggled.

"This, and *How to Live in the New Age*, huh?" Karen laughed.

Donna took the paperback from Karen's hand. She had never even seen a copy of *The Satanic Bible*, although she knew she'd heard about it somewhere.

"Think this would look good next to my *Living Bible*?" Donna teased.

"It's pretty expensive," Karen answered. "You can borrow mine if you want."

"*You* have a copy of *The Satanic Bible*?" she asked in surprise.

"Yeah."

"Why?"

"Why not?" Karen smiled. "It's just another perspective. You want to see it? We can go over to my house."

"Well, uh, sure. It couldn't hurt." Could it?

■

The Satanic Bible was very clear in its principles, and Donna could hardly believe she was actually sitting there, on Karen's bed, reading it. Her mom would faint! She almost laughed when she thought of Pastor Hanley and what he would do if he walked in the door just then.

"Satan represents indulgence, instead of abstinence," Donna read aloud, "and kindness to those who deserve it, instead of love wasted on ingrates."

"It's a little strong," Karen pointed out, "but look at the principle beneath it. It's quite interesting, I think." Then, after a few moments of silence, she asked Donna, "What do you think?"

What would you do?

If Donna gets engrossed, turn to page 30.
If she gets turned off, turn to page 8.

How could it be anything else? Rosalee must have known!
Donna struggled to bring herself back to the issue at hand.

"Mom," she mustered, "I'm really sorry." Donna left the room.
Her mom needed time alone.

That night Donna went over and over every detail of her visit
to Rosalee's tent. She tried not to think about the divorce. Instead,
she concentrated on the powers Rosalee must've used. Donna
wasn't sure if she was afraid or excited, but she knew she had to
know more. She couldn't talk with the kids from church. And
certainly not her mom. Maybe the library would be a good place
to start. Or a bookstore. Donna vaguely remembered a sign
marked "New Age" at her favorite bookstore, and she resolved to
start there and see where it led.

*The Guide to Astrology, Who Were You?—A Guide to Past
Lives, Channeling, Discovering Your Psychic Powers.* There were
so many titles to choose from Donna thought she might have to
make a day of it. She wondered why she'd never noticed the
enormity of the New Age section at this bookstore.

"Can I help you?" The girl in the bookstore smock didn't look
much older than Donna.

"Yes," Donna admitted. "I'm looking for a good book on fortunetelling. Ya know, crystal balls and stuff like that."

"I know a good one," the girl said, and she went straight to
it. *Mystical Practices* was the title, and Donna began reading the
back cover. "*Mystical Practices* delves into another level of life
that, when explored, can provide life-changing insight. Change
your circumstances ... Make life work for you ... Master your
own destiny ..." It seemed to have all the elements she was
looking for.

She purchased the book and hurried down Sixth toward
Cumberland Park.

"A bag of corn chips and a small diet Coke, please," Donna
ordered from a sidewalk vendor. She collected her feast and
walked down the hill.

She stopped beneath a shady tree comfortably removed from
the families and dog-walkers that dotted the park. Donna slid the
book from its bag and carefully opened to the first page.

"The word 'occult' comes from the Latin word 'occultus,' "
she began to read, "and it is defined as things that are mysterious
or secret. Mystical occult practices are the keys that unlock the

mysteries of the world, the unknown things hidden from the average human being."

Donna liked the idea of discovering information not available to just anyone. She soaked up the book's teaching like a thirsty sponge.

When darkness began to drop over the park, Donna still had two chapters to read. She slipped the book back into the bag and headed home. Once at home, she slid the book between the mattress and box spring of her bed.

The weekend slipped past. On Monday morning when Donna headed for school, the book was still hidden in her bed. But on returning home, she was shocked to find the book, sticking out like a neon sign, on top of her bed.

"We need to talk about this, Donna," her mother said from the doorway.

Donna reeled and faced her mother. Her pulse raced, and the inside of her mouth suddenly felt dry and rough.

Blind choice:

Turn to page 13, page 23 or page 45 to discover Mom's reaction.

Donna looked on in amazement. Most parents, she was sure, would be blaming her, not asking forgiveness for their role in all of it.

"Stop it," she finally cried. "Stop it. It's not your fault."

"Oh, Donna," her mom said as she moved closer to her. "It *is* my fault. You wouldn't have gone looking for warmth and acceptance if you'd felt secure at home. I'm responsible for that."

"Dad left us. You didn't leave him." Donna looked her mom in the eye for the first time in a long time. "That's not why I went away anyway. I wanted to find love."

"Honey," her mom sighed, "that church you hooked up with is a cult. They don't serve Jesus there—they serve the pastor. You must know that. If it's the truth you're looking for, you can only find that in Jesus."

Suddenly all the things she'd been hearing for the last three days began to make sense. Donna realized her mother was right. She prayed a silent prayer, thanking God for her mother's persistence and concern.

Then Donna smiled at her mother. "Thanks, Mom," she said.

Donna's mom reached over and took her hand. For the first time Donna understood what real acceptance was. She knew she'd finally found true meaning in her life.

The End

Donna shook the thought from her head. Rosalee had simply ventured a guess and happened to be a bit on target. Donna decided the whole thing was just a coincidence.

"Can I get you anything?" she asked her mom. "Tea or something?"

"Thank you, honey, no," she said through a forced little smile. "I'll be fine. I just need some sleep."

Donna knew her mother wouldn't be doing much sleeping that night, and for that matter, neither would she. What would happen to them now, she wondered. How could this happen?

Donna wanted so much to be comforted, to hear encouraging words, to be hugged. She thought of Bob, always so caring and so willing to lend an ear to her problems. But she imagined he was still feeling upset at her for visiting Rosalee's tent. Bob hadn't approved, and the last thing Donna needed now was a lecture.

She picked up the phone and dialed. "Is Karen there?"

Karen and Donna had become good friends after being paired for a chemistry experiment. Karen was just the sort of person Donna could talk to right now.

"She's not?" Donna asked. "Okay. I'll try her later."

Maybe Bob would feel like talking by the time they met in Sunday school the next morning. Or perhaps she could stop by Karen's after church. She'd decide later.

What would you do?

If Donna talks to Bob, turn to page 10.
If she talks to Karen, turn to page 51.

Donna folded the letter and tucked it safely into her pocket. For weeks, she kept it with her, in the back pocket of her jeans or in the breast pocket of her jacket. She didn't understand why but that letter brought her security.

Over the next few weeks, Donna found it difficult to get into the spirit of things at Evergreen Community, as it was now called. As the group prepared for a Christmas celebration, she noticed the festivities centered around Pastor Wyman instead of Jesus. It was Pastor Wyman's banquet. *His* blessings. *His* Christmas offering. Where was Jesus in all of it? Donna wondered.

Where was Jesus? And just then, Donna touched a hand to her mom's letter. Maybe that's where he was.

"I'll hitchhike if I have to," she said aloud. "But I must go home."

■

The last ride she'd managed to catch brought Donna to her front door.

It was several moments before Donna noticed the bathroom light on, and just as she noticed it, it flicked off. She pictured her mom there, standing in front of the mirror, putting the last hairs in place and spraying that awful-smelling hair spray to keep them just right. Donna longed to smell that smell just then, no matter how much she'd always loathed it before.

"Mom?" Donna called out.

"Donna?" She could hear her mother hurrying down the hall. "Donna? Is that you?"

"Hi, Mom," Donna said meekly.

"Donna!" Mom cried and snatched her daughter by the shoulders and pulled her into a frantic embrace. "Donna! Donna!"

"I'm home, Mom," Donna sobbed. "I'm home."

■

The Christmas Eve service was the best ever for Donna and her mom. As the lights dimmed and the yellow candlelight filled the small church, Donna leaned into her mom and they wrapped their arms tightly around each other.

In the early hours of Christmas morning, just before sunrise, Donna awoke to find her mom sitting in the rocker at the edge of Donna's bed.

"What are you doing?" she asked sleepily.

"Watching you," Mom admitted. "I'm sorry."

"It's okay. I like it. You missed me."

"I did miss you."

"I'm really sorry, Mom," Donna began and then stopped out of emotion.

"Do you know how much I love you?" her mom asked.

Donna reached beneath her pillow and produced the worn, wrinkled letter she'd been saving. "Yes, I do," she sniffed. "I really do. I love you too."

The End

"Mom, it's no big deal," said Donna.

"If you really believed that," Mom reasoned, "you wouldn't have felt the need to hide it."

Donna shifted from one foot to the other and then back again.

"I only hid it so you wouldn't be overly concerned," Donna grinned. "I knew you'd overreact if you saw it. It's just a book."

"Did you buy it? Or borrow it from someone else?"

"I bought it," Donna said softly and then sighed.

Mom straightened. "Why?"

Donna didn't want to answer that question at first, but something inside her said her mother had a right to know, a need to be enlightened. "Remember the day I went to the fair with the youth group?" she began.

"Yes."

"Well, we went into the fortuneteller's tent there," Donna explained. "Just for fun, you know. And this woman, Rosalee, she focused in on me right away and told me all about myself. And then she said something sad was about to happen."

"And that's the night," Mom remembered, "you found out Dad had left."

"Yes!" Donna burst. "So how did she know? How did she know, Mom?" she repeated.

"I don't know, honey," her mom said.

"She has some sort of power," Donna told her. "She knows things the rest of us don't."

"Donna," Mom finally suggested, "why don't you talk to Pastor Hanley about it? I think he just may be able to help. Would you do that?"

"I guess so."

"In the meantime," said Mom, "let's not read any more of this book. Okay?"

"Okay."

Donna gave her mom a big hug. She was relieved at her mom's reaction to finding the book.

■

The following Sunday at the church supper, Donna noticed Pastor Hanley sitting alone at a table in the corner. He was busily working on a piece of Mrs. Letterman's pecan pie.

Do I really want to bring this whole thing up again? thought Donna. Does he have anything new to offer? Donna began to wonder if the whole thing had been overblown. She found herself wringing her hands the way her mom often did.

What would you do?

If she talks to the pastor, turn to page 58.
If she doesn't bring it up, turn to page 69.

The experience at Chaz's house had been so overpowering it was all Donna could think of. Over the weeks, she found herself at the occult bookstore more and more. She spent every spare dollar on materials that could further her knowledge and experience.

She spent far more time and energy studying the occult than her schoolwork, and Donna's bedroom slowly became a treasure-trove of occultic secrets. The space beneath her bed was the place for hiding her books; her socks made perfect jewelry holders for the necklaces and rings her mother could never see.

She pulled more and more away from her mother, blaming her mother's depressive reaction to the divorce. "It's just hard to be around you right now," she told her mom. "I just don't want to think about it."

Donna promptly returned phone calls from Chaz and his group while the phone calls from youth group friends and old friends from school remained unanswered. Bob finally stopped calling after at least a dozen tries at getting together. Donna's interest in church and church functions dropped off soon after her first séance experience. She'd experienced half a dozen more séances since then, and now she wanted to become a witch. She wanted to be an official member of Chaz's black magic coven.

"I couldn't be more pleased," Chaz told her when she shared the news. "Is it your greatest desire?"

"It is," she grinned. "I want to experience the power, I want to learn more. There's a whole world here I never knew existed, and I want my share of it."

"You can never look back," he warned her.

■

Chaz arranged the ceremony, and Donna could hardly wait to get to the clearing in Wentworth Woods that night just before midnight. As she walked toward the clearing, Donna watched the eerie shadows dancing from the fire in the night.

"You'll need to strip," Chaz told her matter-of-factly. "Clothes obstruct the power within you that will be called on."

Donna was reluctant at first, but Chaz convinced her not to let her own modesty stand in the way of what would be the most important night of her life. The coven members carried her to the makeshift altar and set her down, naked, upon it. She found it difficult to focus on the words being spoken.

"Thy blessing," she heard Chaz say over her, above the roar of her own pulse in her ears. "In the pleasures of the flesh and the tranquilities of the mind."

The group around her groaned in unison. "Sustain us, dark lord!"

"For leisure time in pleasure's own pursuit," Chaz cackled toward the sky.

"Sustain us, dark lord!" the group shouted.

Donna thought she might pass out from the adrenalin pulsing through her body. She took a deep breath of the cold night air into her lungs and then coughed out the smoke of whatever was burning in the lamps around her.

"For we are kindred spirits—demon brothers—children of earthly joy," she heard Chaz laugh. "With one voice proclaim, 'So be it! Slava Tchortu!' "

As they repeated them, the words seemed to go right through Donna. "So be it! Slava Tchortu!"

Chaz handed her a chalice to drink from, and the liquid brought her into an indifferent haze. She began to spontaneously laugh as she was symbolically sacrificed to the sun god.

Then Chaz threw a huge cross over her, and she jumped when it crashed to the ground.

She barely knew what had happened when Chaz poked a dagger into the flesh of her wrist. He held her hand over a cup, let some of the blood drain in and then callously, harshly wrapped a cloth around the wound. Someone thrust a pen into her hand and brought a book before her.

"Sign your name," Chaz told her. "In blood. Your new name is Muck Olla, after the sun god. Sign your new name in this, the *Book of Names*."

Donna did as she was told, and at that very moment, she felt something rise inside of her, swelling larger than her own skin, pulsating through every inch of her body. A presence entered her that night, and its voice promised her life would now have new meaning and she would never be the same again.

■

For days following the initiation, Donna experienced drastic changes in her personality.

"Where are you going?" her mother called out to her as

Donna grabbed her jacket and started out the front door.

"None of your business!" a voice snapped out of Donna's throat, and Donna looked back at her mother. Flicking an obscene gesture her mother's way before leaving, Donna smiled at her new-found independence.

Through the headphones that had become a regular part of her garb, Donna sang along. "Sacrifice, oh so nice. Sacrifice to Lucifer, my master. Bring the chalice, raise the knife. Welcome to my sacrifice."

Donna hurried to the secret meeting place in Wentworth Woods. She was the first to arrive after Chaz, and they greeted with their usual warm, impassioned kiss.

"What's on the agenda tonight?" she asked him.

"This!" he snipped, and he hurried to the back of his pickup to produce a burlap potato sack, its contents writhing in a panic.

"What is it?" she inquired.

"Our sacrifice to the master," he snarled. "Our lord requires bloodshed this fine, moonlit night."

Donna shivered a little at the thought of it, but she loved the way Chaz said things, and she tried to focus on him rather than the jumping bundle of life in his grasp.

Meeeooowww!

"A cat," Donna realized aloud, her love for animals rising up into her chest.

"Not a cat," Chaz whispered. "An offering. A blood offering."

"Oh, master of darkness," he screeched as he lifted up the cat over his head, "accept this our sacrifice of thanksgiving to thee, which we do dedicate to thee and to thy legion of demons."

Donna lost herself in the world of smoke whirling around inside her nose. It was a drug of sorts; Chaz called it nightshade. And it burned Donna's nostrils all the way to her brain. But when the dagger went into the animal's abdomen and the squeal of pain raged from its throat, Donna felt herself thrown out of the mindless state into one of sharp awareness and fear.

She fought hard not to vomit afterward, and she couldn't seem to take her eyes off the cat's lifeless little body.

What would you do?

If Donna decides to leave Satanism, turn to page 105.
If she continues to stay involved, turn to page 129.

Donna was glad Karen answered the door. Her smile was a welcome sight, and Donna immediately felt like she'd made the right choice.

"Donna!" Karen greeted her. "What's up?"

"Plenty," Donna tried to smile. "You feel like some company?"

"Absolutely."

Soon the whole story flooded out, and Donna had to admit she felt a lot better after talking.

"I just don't know what's going to happen now," she sighed.

"The important thing," Karen smiled, "is to remember your parents don't control who you are. Each of us is an individual, and we don't need another person to survive. We have within ourselves everything we'll ever need to go on."

Donna wondered if Karen meant that the way it sounded. Where did Jesus fit into that theory?

"You're strong," Karen went on, "You don't need to be rocked or controlled by the decisions of those around you. You can be in control."

It was then Donna noticed the shelf behind Karen's bed. It was dotted with crystalline rocks of different shapes and sizes. Several more of them hung from fish line in the window where they captured the light and sent it splashing across the room in rainbows of magnetic color.

"Here," Karen said as she went to the stereo and flicked a button or two. "Listen to this. It'll help you relax."

Hints and dashes of musical chords made their way around the room. Karen was right; it did help her relax. Donna listened for several minutes as she watched Karen, eyes closed, swaying to the rhythm of the soothing, unconventional music.

"Karen ... "

"Sh," Karen breathed, and Donna waited several moments for the interlude to end and Karen's eyes to flutter open. "Isn't it wonderful?" she cooed.

"This music, the crystals ... " Then Donna asked pointedly: "Are you one of those New Agers?"

Blind choice:
Without looking ahead, turn to page 73 or page 84.

"A séance?" Donna repeated.

"Yeah," Chaz said excitedly. "Be there!"

Chaz was already heading off in the other direction by the time it really hit Donna. "I don't think so, Chaz," she called after him. "I can't."

"Try!" he sang back.

Donna looked down at the book on mystical practices in her hand. She instinctively set the book back on the shelf and headed out the door.

■

"Well, Donna," Pastor Hanley smiled at her from the other side of his desk, "I'm pleased you felt free to come and talk to me about this."

"I wasn't going to," she sighed. "But I'm just so confused."

"The mystery of the occult can be very intriguing," he said. "Especially to someone your age."

"It's getting a little scary," Donna admitted. "The magical part—the power of it—*does* intrigue me. But it seems to lead to ... I mean ... " She trailed off into a sigh that ended in silence.

"The power of the occult is misleading, Donna," he began. "When you play with the occult, *you're* really the one being toyed with. Satan may only have a fraction of God's incredible power, but he's clever—and he knows how to fool people into believing they can be powerful if they follow his ways."

"I just don't get that excited about church," she tried to explain. "It's not as ... as exciting as what Chaz seems to have."

"Dabbling in the occult can be very dangerous," said Pastor Hanley, "because it draws your attention away from the consistent, selfless love of God and into the thrill of the moment. It can also lead you away from God entirely."

"I don't know," Donna replied. "I don't think I could be completely drawn away from God. Not entirely."

"You'd be surprised how quickly it can happen," Pastor Hanley said. "Take your eyes off God's love for a moment, and you can be misled very, very easily. Horoscopes, Ouija boards, occult books, séances—they're all just tools to pull you away from God. Let me read you a scripture passage that might help make sense of this."

Pastor Hanley grabbed his big Bible and skimmed through

the well-used pages. "Here it is—Ephesians 6:12. 'For our struggle is not against flesh and blood, but against the rulers, against the authorities, against the powers of this dark world and against the spiritual forces of evil in the heavenly realms.' "

Pastor Hanley closed his Bible. "I think Paul is talking about the very things you're wondering about."

Donna looked out the window. Was dabbling really dangerous, or was Pastor Hanley wrong?

What would you do?

If she decides dabbling is dangerous, turn to page 125.
If she decides dabbling is harmless, turn to page 83.

"What do you mean why do I play?" Kurt asked seriously, and several other players stopped to hear what he'd say. "D&D is more important than most things I can think of. It's probably the best thing about life. It's exciting, it's incredibly ..."

"Stimulating," one of the other kids finished.

"It seems a little dangerous to me, that's all," Donna told them. "The spiritual parts are bad enough, but what about Kurt's hurt hand? Is that part of the fun? What do you think, Alan?"

She looked around the room, but Alan was already gone. After having made it through the game with the same character since beginning three months ago, Alan's character had been killed that night.

"That's why it's so incredible," Kurt told her. "It's more than a game. We *become* the characters while we play. It's more real than life sometimes."

That scared Donna. She wondered if the game was really harmless or if there would be more far-reaching consequences.

Blind choice:

Without looking ahead, turn to page 12 or page 116.

Donna was one of the first to pile out of the car, and she couldn't help but follow Susan's family into the church. She was intrigued to hear what Susan's pastor would say.

■

Donna and Susan practically flew home from church that Sunday. Their relationship hadn't been strong in years, and Donna was so happy she'd decided to visit Susan's church.

"Your pastor reminds me so much of my pastor," Donna told her that afternoon over lemonade and sugar cookies in Susan's kitchen. "I loved his message on finding Jesus in every book of the Bible. Wasn't it great? Hey ... you know what? Maybe you'd like to visit our church sometime?"

"I'd love it," Susan responded. "I'm so glad we've become friends again, Donna."

"Me too."

"I have this idea," Susan began. "Some of us have been kicking around the idea of an alternative party to Halloween."

"Oh, yeah," Donna cringed. "That holiday is really creeping up on us, isn't it? I wish we didn't even call it a holiday. It's so weird and dangerous."

"And it's such a creepy time. Did you know it's the highest day of honor for Satanists? I think Halloween is just totally evil."

"I don't know about that," Donna said. "But I agree it's turned into a real dangerous holiday."

"Well, anyway, what if we worked together with both our churches and made it a community thing?"

"I think it'd be great!" Donna exclaimed.

■

Susan and Donna mapped out every detail at least a dozen times. The recreation center donated the hall. Merchants from all over town had come through with soft drinks, baked goods, pizza, toys—even decorations. Susan and Donna orchestrated a huge and exciting treasure hunt for the older children, and there were enough games scheduled to keep younger children entertained for the whole evening. Everything they needed to make the party a smash was there—except the people.

Donna checked her watch for the fourth time. "7:20," she announced.

"Yes, I know!" Susan snapped. "First 7:17, then 7:18, and 7:19 ... I figured 7:20 would be next. Would you relax a little? The party doesn't start until 8."

"Sorry," Donna offered. "I guess I'm a little wired."

"Come on," Susan suggested. "Help me bring out a few more jugs of apple cider."

"What if no one shows up?" Donna groaned as they headed off.

"Then we'll have a major feast tonight," Susan answered stiffly.

"I'm serious, Susan," said Donna. "What if nobody comes?"

Blind choice:

Without looking ahead, turn to page 87 or page 123 to find out if the party is a success.

"It's bizarre!" she called back without looking up from the book. "I can't believe this stuff came from Bob. He's so careful about anything that doesn't seem to be in line with the Bible. This stuff all sounds so New Age."

"New Age, huh?" Mom walked over and glanced at the book her daughter was reading. "Maybe you ought to talk to Bob about these books."

"I was thinking of showing them to Pastor Hanley, first," Donna suggested. "What do you think?"

"It sure couldn't hurt."

■

"I hope you don't mind my taking up your time, Pastor Hanley," Donna said from the other side of the big oak desk.

"Certainly not," he assured her. "That's what I'm here for."

"Have you had a chance to look at the books I gave you?"

"Yes, I have."

Blind choice:

Without looking ahead, turn to page 99 or page 104 to see how Pastor Hanley responds.

"Pastor Hanley?" she said. "Can I talk to you?"

"Certainly," he beamed at her as he wiped a few flakes of pie crust from his mouth.

"When the youth group went to the fair," she began, "we went into the tent of Rosalee the Seer, this gypsy with a crystal ball."

Pastor Hanley set down his paper cup on the table in front of him. She had his full attention.

"She told me things," Donna went on. "Things she couldn't have known."

"Like what, Donna?"

"Like that I would go home that night, and my dad would have left us."

"She told you that?"

"Well," Donna admitted, "not in so many words. But she told me something very sad was about to happen. And then I found out my dad had already left. She knew. But that's not what I wanted to talk to you about. I bought this book—*Mystical Practices*—and it tells about all these powers—like what Rosalee used. Anyway, my mom found it and she's worried. She says it's a really dangerous and terrible thing. I think it's just a book. You know?"

"Anything having to do with the occult, Donna, can be dangerous. And things such as fortunetelling, horoscopes and books on mystical practices are part of the occult world. Jesus said, 'You can't eat at my table and at Satan's table too.' When you begin to explore these kinds of things, you're looking for trouble. It's just not possible to serve God and dabble in the occult too."

"But we all do it," Donna rationalized. "Lots of people read their horoscopes or have their fortunes told. It's an innocent game. It's not like we're turning away from God when we do it."

"It's not?" Pastor Hanley asked gently. "After you went to see Rosalee, what did you do? Didn't you go and buy a book to learn more? As far as everyone doing it, Donna, remember the scripture that says it's our responsibility to expose the things of darkness? Perhaps the next time you see someone stepping into a dangerous area, you might consider confronting the problem rather than joining in."

Donna didn't know how to respond. She thanked Pastor Hanley and walked over to the dessert table.

Just that moment, Donna saw Carrie Bartholomew heading out the door with her two younger sisters. Donna had overheard

Carrie talking that morning in the girls room about someone at her school who told fortunes by reading tarot cards.

Donna thought about Pastor Hanley's advice. Should she confront Carrie about it or leave it alone? But then, who was she to talk? She had a book called *Mystical Practices* on the night stand at home!

Donna watched a few more moments as Carrie helped one of her sisters into her jacket.

What would you do?

If she talks with Carrie, turn to page 81.
If she leaves Carrie alone, turn to page 88.

Kidnapping a baby wasn't going to be as easy as they'd thought, so the group, prompted by Chaz, began discussing an alternative sacrifice to Satan. Donna listened with great interest as her once-close-friend Susan was suggested as an option. Ultimately, Susan became the chosen one because of her apparent innocence and because of her allegiance to the enemy church. Luring her out to the woods was almost too simple.

■

It wasn't murder, Donna kept insisting. It was a sacrifice to the master. "Just like Abraham," she cried. "He was going to sacrifice his son to his God. We do that too. It's part of our religion. It's not murder!"

But the judge didn't see it that way, and Donna, Chaz and the six others involved were all locked up to await their trials. The judge had found Donna's argument so appalling, in fact, he ruled she and Chaz would face trial for their crimes as adults. Both were sentenced to lifelong prison terms.

■

Donna could seldom keep her mind occupied in that cell. Her thoughts drifted from her mother's face when she'd come to the prison, to the judge's booming voice when he told the courtroom how appalling and emotionless Donna was.

She tried to meditate, but she couldn't get her mind to remain quiet long enough. She tried to read, but the words melted together into a mishmash of print over print.

Every night Donna recited the incantation she believed would eventually bring her freedom. And every morning, as she awoke in the familiar cold, impersonal surroundings, she cried as her hope slowly dissolved.

She couldn't understand it. Her powers had always been so real, so fruitful. But not now. Where was Satan now when she really needed him?

The End

"Yes," she answered thoughtfully. "The book suggests ways to make the divorce more comfortable for the child caught in the middle."

"That sounds interesting," Mom commented as she headed out of the room. "I hope it helps, honey."

Donna settled back to take a look at the video. Comments by the psychologist followed dramatic scenes of actual counseling sessions. He described how every mountain is climbable if the person takes care of him- or herself first.

"In the midst of a crisis," he told Donna through the television, "your last priority will be yourself. You'll be thinking about that friend who's in financial trouble, your parents who are divorcing, your brother facing illness. You cannot have a victory over stress or anything else without first focusing on what *you* need."

Donna liked what Dr. Viscrow had to say. He addressed her personal needs, her desires and her troubles. No one else seemed to do that.

She watched Dr. Viscrow's video twice and then devoured the paperback book written by him. She felt stronger that night. And happier. She realized she'd been neglecting herself. She resolved to go on a healthy eating plan, to construct an exercise regimen and to get some vitamins.

The relaxation techniques she learned were also effective, and every night before she went to bed, she turned on the cassette tape of ocean waves and sea gulls that lulled her into readiness to relax her toes, then her feet and then her ankles.

∎

When the youth group came together on Sunday morning, Donna could hardly wait to thank Bob for the tapes and books.

"So, they helped you," Bob smiled. "That's great!"

"What's helped you?" Kevin seemed to have a knack for walking in halfway through conversations.

"Some tapes and books Bob loaned me," Donna told him. "My folks are getting a divorce."

"A divorce?" Laura repeated. "Why didn't you tell us?"

None of the kids noticed Tim Benson standing at the front of the room, skimming through his Bible.

"So what were these tapes all about?" Laura inquired.

"Coping," Donna told her. "They focus on the kid's pain in a crisis. And they teach relaxation techniques and eating habits that help ease the pain."

"What kind of relaxation techniques?" Laura asked.

"Simple breathing. Listening to music and relaxing your body one part at a time."

"Isn't that New Age?" Shari suggested, and Lisa, the new girl, nodded behind her.

"I wouldn't give Donna New Age tapes!" Bob snapped. "These tapes just help you relax."

"Well, it sounds like meditation to me," Shari countered.

"So," Bob said. "Meditation isn't bad."

"He's right," Kevin chimed in. "It's just a way to take it slow after a busy day."

"Meditation is even in the Bible," Bob insisted. "In Genesis, Isaac meditated."

"Show us," Shari insisted. "I'll bet you'll find he was meditating on God's Word."

"Genesis," Bob mumbled as he made his way quickly through his Bible. "Here! Chapter 24, verse ... 63. 'He went out to the field one evening to meditate.' See?"

"Tim, is that right?" Shari questioned. "This isn't the same kind of meditation Bob's talking about, is it?"

Everyone looked over at Tim, their Sunday school teacher and youth director.

"Well, it's partly right, Shari," he explained. "I don't think you'll find in the Bible a man or woman of God meditating unless it's on godly things. The word 'meditation' has taken on a new meaning over the last few decades."

"Okay," Bob conceded. "It's different. That doesn't mean it's wrong."

"It leads to other stuff," Shari argued.

"Like channeling?" Donna laughed. "Can you guys see me channeling?"

"I'll bet Shirley MacLaine might've said that once too," Laura grinned.

"Well, it's something to think about," Tim said. "Let's hear from the rest of the class? Any other feelings?"

The discussion pre-empted whatever Tim had prepared for that day. Donna listened intently, but offered very little input. She wondered if meditation really was a New Age trap or if it was a viable way of relaxing.

What would you do?

If Donna decides to keep using the relaxation techniques, turn to page 27.

If she stops using them, turn to page 94.

Donna had never met a pastor as captivating as Pastor Wyman. He was strikingly handsome and quite young compared to her own pastor.

"God sent me here on a mission," he told them as he concluded his teaching on accountability, "and I am blessed and humbled at being ordained as your leader and teacher. I want you all to know how much I've come to love you in Christ, and I praise God for this divine commission to be in authority over such loving, giving, God-fearing people."

Pastor Wyman impressed Donna; he was a dynamic leader.

"Well, I used to feel that way too," Donna heard one member say to another, "until Pastor Wyman made it clear that what it actually meant was ..." The voice trailed off as Donna and Susan headed out the front door.

Donna could see that everyone respected and revered Pastor Wyman—even the youth group members.

"What did you think of Pastor Wyman?" Susan asked Donna. "Isn't he incredible?"

"Yes," she replied.

"I hope you'll come back again," offered David, the guy Donna and Susan sat with in Sunday school.

"Yes," another boy added.

"Come back again, Donna!" a girl named Kathy chimed in. "Maybe you'd like to come with Susan to the Wednesday night teaching."

Donna felt welcome and loved at Susan's church. Warmth radiated from everyone she met. Donna was surprised to see how much people accepted Susan. No one seemed to notice Susan's odd clothes or her too-short hair or those little round glasses. They accepted Susan as if she were just like any one of them, and she responded to their treatment with an openness and confidence Donna couldn't remember seeing in Susan during all the years she'd known her.

"Susan told us your parents are going through a divorce," David said as they walked out to the parking lot. "Some of us have gone through the same thing. Maybe we could clear it with Pastor Wyman to start a support group. Would you be interested in something like that?"

Donna admitted she would. Until that moment, she'd felt like no one on earth could understand what she was going through, and it was reassuring to know there were others who'd actually survived it.

"Maybe we could get together one night this week at my house," Donna suggested.

"Well, we couldn't do that," David explained. "Not unless you join the church, anyway."

"What?" Donna was puzzled.

"It's nothing against you," David grinned. "Pastor Wyman just frowns on us meeting outside of the church. He likes us to share our emotions and feelings exclusively with him or with other members of the congregation. He says there's nothing for us out there in the world—only here, in this place that God has provided for us."

"Oh." It seemed to Donna that Pastor Wyman's authority over the church was more far-reaching than she'd first observed.

That afternoon Donna told her mom all about the visit to Susan's church, about Pastor Wyman and about how unusually confident and outgoing Susan seemed there. Then Donna explained the strange response David had to her suggestion of a meeting at her house.

"You mean they wouldn't come over to the house unless you joined the church?" Donna's mom inquired. "That sounds a little odd."

"David said Pastor Wyman doesn't like them to look for comfort anywhere besides in the church."

"Doesn't that sound a little bit out of balance to you?"

"Oh, Mom . . ." Donna began.

"I mean it, Donna," Mom went on. "I can't judge the church or the people there, but it sure sounds like a very controlling situation. Almost like a cult."

"David suggested forming some sort of support group for kids with parents going through divorce," Donna interrupted. "That's how the whole subject came up."

"Well, that's a pretty good idea," her mom encouraged. "Why don't you start something like that at our church?"

Donna's face dropped. She didn't find the idea of starting a group in her own church as appealing as spending time with Susan's friends. Maybe it was the concern she'd felt from David that was drawing her to Susan's church. Or perhaps it was simply his soft brown eyes.

"Honey, you aren't going to stop attending our church, are you?"

"I don't know," Donna admitted. "I love our church. But I feel more comfortable with the kids at Susan's church than with the kids at our church. I'd like to visit Susan's church for a while."

"Donna, are you sure about this?" Mom asked.

What would you do?

If Donna decides she wants to attend Susan's church, turn to page 90.

If she decides to avoid Susan's church, turn to page 121.

"I'd like to organize our own group," Donna told them. "And design it to reach kids just like us who are attracted to New Age ideas."

"I'm with Donna," Bob smiled. "Where do we start?"

"We start," said Yvette, "with a discussion of what attracts kids to the New Age movement."

"I think the mystery or the promise of self-fulfillment is the first attraction," Donna suggested. "Then I think it's the concern for our world. Ecology. The ozone. The Christian church doesn't seem to be as concerned about that stuff as New Agers."

"I don't think that's true," Dane defended. "It's just not as important an issue as, say, alcohol or drug abuse. But it's a good point."

"Maybe we could address the issue of the environment," Yvette offered. "We could sponsor meetings that offer discussions on world peace and on caring for God's creation."

"Exactly!" said Donna. "That's exactly it!"

"We could make fliers and go to other churches, maybe even approach a few New Age groups and invite them to join us," added Dane.

The plans moved so fast they planned the first three meetings in less than an hour and set the date for the first session. Donna and Dane volunteered to be in charge of sending out invitations to three different New Age groups.

Blind choice:

Without looking ahead, turn to page 34 or page 112 to find out whether the outreach group makes a difference.

"It's a support group," she admitted.

"A support group," Mom repeated. "Supporting what?"

"Spiritual awareness."

"What does that mean?" her mom asked seriously.

"Mom, they focus on things the church just doesn't even touch on," Donna explained. "Like the inner searching and longing for answers. And they're real concerned about the environment. Our church doesn't do half the stuff these people do to make our world a better place. The church is so one-dimensional to me. It's so rigid and unbending."

"Honey, the laws of the Bible are rigid because they were issued by God. We don't question them for that reason. But that's the legalistic view of Christianity. There's a far more exciting side. The side that includes the love Jesus has for his children, the grace we've been given, the forgiveness at every turn. If you aren't getting that out of Christianity, you're missing something."

"Then I'm missing something I guess," Donna said softly.

"Have you talked to anyone at church about these feelings?"

"Well, no."

"Why don't you go to that Christian Concerns group next week? I've heard they have some great discussions about the kinds of things you're questioning."

What would you do?

If Donna visits the Christian Concerns group, turn to page 101.

If she sticks with her New Age group, turn to page 127.

"Hello, Donna." Pastor Hanley must've noticed her staring at him.

"Hi, Pastor," she answered.

"Having a good time today?" he asked.

"Yeah," she told him. "I ate too much though."

Pastor Hanley chuckled at that and Donna smiled. She loved his laugh.

"Have a seat. Something on your mind?"

Donna paused. Am I that transparent? she wondered. She thought he might be seeing right into her, and it made her nervous. "No, nothing," she finally responded. "I have to be heading home. I have a science project due tomorrow."

"Oh, well," Pastor Hanley nodded. "Don't let me keep you from your education. A mind's a terrible thing to waste, you know."

"Well, see you later," Donna sighed. Without looking back, she headed out into the fresh air.

Donna felt unusually happy as she walked back to her house. There's so much out there in the world, she thought. So much to be discovered.

Donna wanted to see and feel everything life had to offer, especially at that moment. God had given her a universe of sights and sounds and tastes to experience, and she was sure he'd encourage her to embrace the adventures that lay ahead.

On the way home, Donna crossed over Brand Avenue and took the long way around past the new bookstore in town. She stopped outside and slid two quarters in the machine out front. A rolled paper popped to the surface, and Donna snatched it out of the compartment.

Next month's horoscope. Libra. Just for fun.

"You'll find true love this month. But beware of friends who might mislead you," read Donna.

Friends who might mislead? Donna wondered. Who would try to mislead me? Then she laughed aloud. "What am I worried about? It's just a horoscope."

■

The slumber party at Karen's that weekend was just a ruse to get Donna out of the house without her mom knowing. Karen had invited Donna to join a group of her friends at a Halloween street party being held in Karen's neighborhood. Everyone was to come in costume. Donna tucked her put-together gypsy costume inside her overnight bag on top of an extensive makeup kit and pointed satin shoes she'd picked up at the thrift store.

At Karen's house, Donna had no sooner finished the final touches on her costume when she heard the front doorbell ring. Karen's friends had arrived.

Donna hardly knew anyone there. Goblins, witches, ghosts and vampires joined the gypsies and cowboys that headed out across Gaylord Avenue toward State Street.

Donna noticed that one of the houses was decorated as a haunted house—complete with flickering candles and scary music. There was so much food Donna thought she'd pop after about two hours of moving from one table to another and from one candy dish to another, each household providing a different treat.

"We have the best neighborhood association in the city!" Karen told Donna over the blare of the music. "Is this great, or what?!"

"This is all too tame for me," one of Karen's friends said through his demon mask. "How about we get down to some serious D&D?"

Donna turned to Karen. "D&D?"

"Dungeons & Dragons," she clarified. "It's the greatest game—kind of like the make-believe games kids play—only lots better. You in?"

"Sure. Why not!"

"It's a role-playing game," Alan, the vampire, explained as they walked back across Gaylord. "Each character has six abilities determined by the roll of the dice. Intelligence, dexterity, charisma, strength, wisdom and constitution. Kurt is our Dungeon Master, and he'll lead us every step of the way. His job is to create situations for us to respond to as characters in an imaginary world. Why don't you watch for a while, Donna. You'll catch on."

It took Donna only a few minutes to discover D&D was more than just a game. It was a hobby! Most of the players knew their spells and incantations of protection by heart. She noticed Kurt referring to a couple of books and an occasional chart as he led the various characters on their imaginary journey.

Donna picked up one of the books and read the first thing

her eyes fell upon. "Serving a deity is a significant part of D&D," she read to herself, "and all player characters should have a patron god. Alignment assumes its full importance when tied to the worship of a deity."

"I call upon the mighty emperor of the night!" Alan called out. "Your assistance please, oh imperial one, Tramus, spirit of the battle." Donna, startled, automatically slapped the book down where it was.

Alan was calling upon a demon spirit, Donna realized, and she began to watch the other players gathered around the table. Their eyes were open, but they saw another world, thought Donna, an imaginary world that seemed dangerously real. They played out the action in their minds as clearly as any battle Donna had ever watched on television.

■

It was after midnight when Kurt's parents wandered into the family room to break up the game and send the players on their way.

"So what do you think of D&D?" Kurt asked Donna as they were clearing out.

"Pretty intense," she replied.

"It is that," he said with a smile. "We've had this game in progress for three months now."

"Three months! Is it always ... like it was tonight?"

Kurt laughed. "I nearly lost a hand the last time we played." And he held out his hand to Donna, a mass of stitches and flesh not quite healed.

"How?"

"My own fault, I guess," he chuckled. "We were all so into the game, none of us knows exactly how it happened!"

"It's so consuming. Why do you play it, Kurt?" Donna asked. "What's the point?"

Blind choice:

Without looking ahead, turn to either page 54 or page 93 to discover Kurt's answer.

"A New Ager?" Karen retorted.

"Well, the music is definitely ... " Donna began.

"This stuff?" she asked. "It's meditative."

"And the crystals?"

"Quartz crystals," Karen said. "My dad's brother is a geologist, and he's been adding to my collection since I was 4 years old. And besides, what's so bad about crystals?"

Donna waved her hand in surrender. "I'm sorry. I guess I'm overly aware, that's all."

"Aware of what?"

"At church we've been learning about how the New Age movement can be very inviting through little things like crystals, music and theories about people having everything they need inside them to succeed."

"Oh, that's right, you're a Christian," Karen remembered. "I'm not against Christianity, Donna. I just don't think that's all there is to life."

"That's the danger of the New Age movement," began Donna. "The practices and the beliefs lead the follower away from the teachings of the Bible, and ... "

"How do you know?" Karen smiled. "If you're a Christian, how do you know what New Agers believe?"

"My youth director did a series of meetings on it a few weeks ago, and ... "

"And he taught you to be careful of those crystal-carrying, music-listening New Agers out there," she scoffed, "or they might hurt you or corrupt you before you even know it."

"Karen, I'm serious," Donna tried to explain.

"I know," she laughed, "but I just can't take what you have to say all that seriously. I don't believe taking ideas from lots of religions can harm you; I think it can only enrich your way of thinking."

"New Age thinking isn't dangerous," Karen continued. "It's just different from what you believe—it's broader, bigger in scope, than your Christianity. You see, I don't dismiss other religion's beliefs like you Christians do. I figure we can even learn from Satanists."

"Satanists!" Donna exclaimed. "Now, they really are different from me. Way different!"

"Different, yes," Karen reasoned. "But not dangerous."

"I'm sorry, Karen," Donna tried to explain, "but I can't agree with ..."

"Look!" Karen reached under her bed and produced a black, leather-bound book with worn, gold lettering across the front and a faded diagram of a star inside a circle.

It was the satanic bible.

"You're a Satanist?" Donna gasped.

"No, silly!" Karen smiled. "But that doesn't mean I can't look into their bible and see what they believe, or even practice some of their ways. It won't bite, Donna. Take it!"

Donna took the book and set it down on the bed beside her. Karen reached over and randomly flipped it open and said, "Look at it. It can't hurt you."

Donna turned to the beginning of the book. She landed on "The Nine Satanic Statements." She scanned quickly over them.

"Satan represents indulgence, instead of abstinence ... Satan represents kindness to those who deserve it, instead of love wasted on ingrates ... Satan represents all of the so-called sins, as they all lead to physical, mental or emotional gratification ..."

It was all so new and different from the teachings Donna had learned in her church and from her Christian family.

"So, what do you think?" Karen finally asked.

What would you do?

If Donna gets engrossed, turn to page 30.
If Donna is turned off, turn to page 8.

Before she could respond, Chaz grabbed her by the hair and yanked so hard she cried out. He dragged her across the living room floor like a rag doll, the others following close behind. Someone picked up her feet and helped carry her out the front door while someone else ripped at her clothing.

It was hard to keep track of what was happening, and Donna frantically struggled to free herself from whatever it was they had bound her with. Slamming doors, a moving car, squealing tires. It was impossible to think. Too much was happening. She just wanted to break free, to wake up from this nightmare, to escape Chaz and the sadistic laughter that echoed in her ears.

She was relieved when the car came to a stop, but Donna winced in pain as Chaz and his friends dragged her from the car and rolled her on the ground. Donna felt something wet and sticky pouring over her body. Hands upon hands rubbed the goop all over her. Then Chaz leaned over her and sneered at her as he tried to get a grip on her slimy body.

Something horrible ... what was it? Donna suddenly realized they were rolling her in animal manure, which was sticking to the honey that had been rubbed over every inch of her half-naked body.

Another reeling trip in the car and Donna felt herself propelled from the moving car. She felt the sickening thud as her skull collided with the pavement. Everything went dark.

The next thing Donna remembered was when she woke up in the hospital.

"Mom?"

Her mom was at her side in an instant, holding her hand and looking down at her.

"What happened?" she asked as her head cleared.

"Oh, honey," her mom whispered. "Just rest, Donna. You need to get some rest."

During the following days, Donna slipped in and out of consciousness. She sensed tiny fractions of her mother's visits, but large blocks of time slipped away from her.

Finally, she began to recognize the pain she felt in her bruised and broken body, she felt herself fighting to become human again. On one particular evening, she finished a meal and promptly dozed off, only to be startled out of her restful sleep by the familiar ring of a telephone.

"Hello," she managed sleepily.

"Donna?"

"Yes."

"Donna, you're not going to walk away. We'll finish you off. You can't just walk away."

"Who is this? Rhonda?"

"You'll never live to tell the tale."

Donna slammed the receiver down into the cradle so hard she thought it might've cracked. A shiver of fear scrambled up her back.

Once she'd left the hospital, the phone calls began in earnest. In the following weeks, Donna experienced that same shiver many times. Every time the phone rang, she jumped, knowing it would probably be another harassing phone call.

Upon returning home from church one Sunday, Donna noticed something on the doorstep leaning up against the front door. As she approached it, that same shiver, only more intense, more overpowering, made its way up her back. A doll, made of straw and burlap—a childish replica of Donna—was lying against her front door with long, straight hatpins protruding from it. Beside the doll lay a note. Scrawled in blood across the torn piece of paper were the words, "You can run—but you can't hide."

"What am I going to do, Mom?" she asked over tea at the kitchen table. "I can't take this anymore!"

"No," Mom sighed. "Neither can I."

"It's just got to stop!" Donna sobbed. "Mom, can't we move away or something? Can't we just go somewhere else and start over? I want to go someplace where no one knows us or what I've done in the past. I want to start again."

"Now that the divorce is nearly final," her mom began, "I must say that sounds appealing to me too."

They exchanged hopeful smiles.

"We could start a whole new life," encouraged Donna.

"I've always wanted to see Canada."

"Canada? Yeah!" Donna smiled.

"Let's hear it for the great adventurers," her mom laughed. "Just you and me, God's guidance and the big world."

"A whole new life," Donna promised herself and her mom. As Donna hugged her mom, she felt safe and happy for the first time in months.

The End

Two weeks passed. Donna was surprised her mother or the police hadn't come after her. It was almost a relief when a letter finally found its way to her. Donna held it close to her before opening it. She was almost afraid to read it.

Dear Donna,

I don't know if you'll ever get this letter, but I had to write it anyway. I was thinking back to a time when we used to sit on your bed until far too late into the night and tell each other secrets and laugh until we cried.

I miss you. And I miss our times together.

I don't agree with what you've done, Donna. I think you know that. And I want you back home with all my heart. But I know you feel strongly about Susan's church.

Please think carefully about what you've done. Pray about it.

And no matter what, know I love you—very much. Honey, you're everything to me, and I miss you so much.

You'll always be welcome here, Donna. I hope you'll come home.

Love,
Mom

Donna wondered how her mom had found out where to send the letter. She couldn't help reading the letter over and over again, and she smiled at the way her mom had signed her name, with a little heart next to it.

Donna admitted to herself she missed her mom. She missed her mom's french toast and the way she'd hum when she was working around the house. But the thought of going back was another issue.

Donna had found a new family now—and new meaning in her life.

Donna read the letter again. "You'll always be welcome here, Donna."

What would you do?

If Donna returns home to her mom, turn to page 43.
If she stays, turn to page 19.

Donna leaned over toward Bob. "What do you think?" she whispered.

A quick glare from the woman in front of them prevented Bob from responding, and Donna sank back into her seat.

"Life as we know it is being corrupted!" Leland warned.

■

Donna received Leland's call to arms like a true soldier! She walked away from the seminar feeling newly enlightened and strengthened by what she'd learned. She couldn't wait to tell her friends.

"I can't believe you fell for all that!" Karen retorted.

"What do you mean?" Donna asked. "How can you not see it?"

"How can you try and explain it all away so simply?" Karen argued over the crunch of Oreo cookies.

"Because it *is* so simple," Donna explained. "Good intentions and cosmic spiritual awakening won't make our lives meaningful. Only a relationship with God can do that."

Karen didn't respond. Instead, she looked off into the distance, as if bored by Donna's "sermon."

"You know what your problem is?" Donna asked.

"Do tell."

"You just can't grasp the idea someone could love you the way Jesus loves you. Completely and unconditionally."

Karen turned and looked into Donna's eyes with burning intensity.

Blind choice:

Without looking ahead, turn to page 107 or page 119 to find out if Karen accepts or rejects Donna's views.

She liked the idea of joining the church. Everyone had treated her so warmly, so much like part of the family already, she couldn't think of a better place to declare her desire to be a part of them.

"Yes," Donna grinned. "That would be a perfect time."

At the service the following day, Kathy and Susan stood with Donna as her sponsors, and she declared her intention to loyally serve the church. She offered her watch—once worn by her great grandmother—as a token of her dedication. Pastor Wyman gratefully accepted it.

"Our God has brought us a wonderful gift in Donna," he told the congregation. "Let's pray he sends more like her. More with her spirit and servanthood."

Hordes of members moved in around Donna with hugs and kisses and pats on the back.

"Welcome!" they all greeted her, and she felt more loved just then than she'd ever felt in her life.

■

During the coming weeks, Donna began to see more and more why the church members had so much faith in their leader Pastor Wyman. He was a strong, inspired man of God. Whenever someone had a problem or concern, Pastor Wyman would counsel them with words he'd been given by God for that particular situation.

"We're moving!" Pastor Wyman announced one morning as he took his place at the podium. "We're going to follow God into the 'promised land,' my dear people. He is leading us to a new place—a place in the desert. Fifty acres of worship and fellowship with God."

It was the talk of the church, and no one seemed to have anything bad to say about the intended move. Susan's family put their house up for sale immediately, and people began making plans to pool their finances and follow the leading of God that Pastor Wyman had presented.

"I want us to go with them, Mom," Donna had pleaded. "Please. It will be so beautiful!"

But Donna couldn't get through to her mom. So she made her own plans. She'd leave with Susan's family.

Just a few weeks later, Donna sat at the kitchen table, hastily writing a letter to her mom. Susan's family was waiting outside—anxious to begin the long trip to Pastor Wyman's promised land.

> Dear Mom,
>
> Don't worry about me, I'll be fine. I've gone to live where God has called me. He has a plan for me there, and I must follow his leading. I'll always love you, Mom, but I have to go.
>
> Love,
> Donna

As Donna walked out the door, she turned back and snapped a mental picture of her house. This is the toughest decision I've ever made, she thought. But I know it's the right decision.

A moment later, she was gone.

Blind choice:

Without looking ahead, turn to page 20 or page 77 to see how Donna's mother reacts.

Expose the things of darkness. The words sang in Donna's ears as she hurried across the fellowship hall toward the door.

"Carrie!" Donna called.

The brilliant sunlight caught Carrie's red hair as she turned.

"Hi, Donna! What's up?"

"I wanted to talk to you about something," she said casually. "I heard you talking to Rae and Sharon this morning about having your tarot cards read at school."

"Yeah," Carrie grinned. "It's great. I'm going to learn how to do it too, and then I can read yours."

"Well ..." Donna didn't know how to go on. A lump rose in her throat the size of a grapefruit. "I was reminded of the scripture that says we can't eat at the Lord's table and at Satan's table too, and ... uh ..."

"Oh, pleeease," Carrie groaned. "Don't tell me you're going to jump on my case for having my fortune read! I heard *you* went into the fortuneteller's tent at the fair."

"I did," Donna admitted. "But I know I was wrong."

"Donna, I'll tell you what," Carrie patronized, "you take care of you, and I'll take care of me. Okay?"

Carrie didn't wait for an answer. She turned abruptly and was out the church door.

"Oh, that was just great!" Donna groaned aloud.

"You and Carrie have a problem?"

Donna turned to find Tim, her youth director, standing behind her.

"Hi, Tim," she tried to smile. "I was just talking to Carrie about something Pastor Hanley was talking with me about," she hesitated.

"And?"

"It didn't go over too well. I really don't feel qualified in talking about this kind of stuff—you know, the occult and all that—especially since I'm probably just as curious as Carrie is about it all."

Tim smiled and put his arm around Donna's shoulder. "There's a seminar next Saturday you might be interested in. About New Age beliefs and how they've crept into society. Would you like to go?"

"Yes!" Donna said excitedly. "The next time I talk to someone about this stuff, I think I'd better have more facts."

■

When Donna arrived at the seminar, she noticed Bob waiting to go in.

She and Bob slipped into their seats just two chairs behind Tim and his wife Grace, who turned and smiled at them just as Leland Craine, the main speaker, stepped up to the podium.

"I want to talk to you today about something very, very dangerous," Leland said staunchly into the microphone. "The New Age. The New Age is the devil's conspiracy that's taking over every single walk of life. No one is safe. Not our children or our grandchildren. Not our young adults. Not our senior citizens. We're all under siege."

Donna and Bob exchanged dramatic looks as Leland paused and looked into the faces dotted throughout the room.

"Karma!" he shouted. "Teachings of reincarnation, channeling, the occult! Astrology, tarot cards, lotions, potions, spells and so-called white witchcraft! In the news, nearly every day, we hear someone speak of a supposedly peaceful one-world order. This is a New Age ideal. There's no escape. No escape except, that is, for understanding. And that's why I'm here with you today. I want to arm you for battle with the weapon of knowledge!"

Donna squirmed in her chair. She hadn't expected such a strong anti-New Age message. Was Leland Craine on target? Or was he way off base? she wondered.

She listened carefully to the rest of his message.

What would you do?

If Donna accepts Leland Craine's perspective, turn to page 78.
If she rejects his perspective, turn to page 37.

Donna didn't want to hurt Pastor Hanley's feelings, but she was pretty sure he was overreacting. Horoscopes and Ouija boards were harmless fun. Everyone knew that. She wasn't so sure about séances though.

Donna looked at her pastor and tried to smile. He was a nice enough man and she respected him, and yet she just couldn't swallow what he had to say.

"I'm going to have to go," she said as politely as she could manage. "I really appreciate your seeing me though. Thanks for listening."

"Any time," he answered.

■

"Can I have the horoscopes?"

Donna couldn't help but think of Pastor Hanley when she said it, and she smiled as Lucy handed her a page from the center of the school newspaper. She quickly scanned it and landed on the forecast for Libra.

"It says here this will be my best week yet in terms of grades," Donna announced to her friends at the lunch table. "And I'm going to meet someone very romantic who'll change my life forever! I hope it's that new guy who transferred in from Washington."

"David Weigand?" Carly cried. "He's going to change *my* life, not yours!"

"Not according to this," Donna grinned, waving the page of horoscopes over her head. "You're a Virgo, aren't you? It says here your love life will hit a new low this week."

"Ugh!" Carly moaned.

"Do you follow your horoscopes? Faithfully, I mean?"

Donna looked up to find a new girl, Tanya, looking at her seriously. She couldn't tell whether Tanya was asking out of curiosity or whether she was expressing the slightest hint of condemnation.

"They're all for fun," Donna shrugged. "What's your sign? I'll read yours."

Blind choice:
Without looking ahead, turn to either page 7 or page 114.

"I don't like labels," Karen smiled. "I prefer to simply say I'm enlightened."

"Then you don't believe in God?" Donna inquired gently.

"I do," Karen corrected, "I believe in God. Perhaps not in the same form you believe, but I know there's a higher power. An energy. A force of nature."

"And where does the Bible fit in?" Donna asked curiously.

"The Bible is a wonderful part of history," Karen explained. "It tells of our ancestry, the beliefs of our forefathers. I like reading it. It shows me how far we've come, how many roads we've traveled as human beings. There's a wonderful verse in the New Testament about being able to move mountains if only you believe you can. That's the key to the mysteries of the universe. We can do anything if we only believe. And look at this world. It's in such a mess—we need to do something about it. I don't see Christians doing anything to stop pollution or clean up the environment."

"Belief in ourselves," Karen continued, "is the key to everything. Knowing what strength we have inside ourselves creates a power that can do anything!"

"Believing in yourself is important," Donna told her. "But I believe you need a relationship with Christ to find meaning in life."

Karen's enthusiasm deflated. "We're each responsible for our own destiny. That's the way it works. I think it's dangerous to give the responsibility for our lives to someone else. *Christianity* is dangerous."

"The danger isn't in Christianity," Donna said softly. "The danger is in misunderstanding scripture. Someone taught you the verse about moving mountains means belief in yourself. What the scripture actually says is mountains can be moved through faith in God."

"The wonderful thing about Christianity," Donna carefully explained, "is there is someone willing to take responsibility for us—someone who loves us so much he became a sacrifice for our sins."

"Jesus," Karen interrupted. "I paid attention in Sunday school way back when. I just don't believe it can be that easy."

"It *is* that easy," Donna smiled. "That's the beauty of it. All it takes is asking God to become part of your life. And the best part is God really wants us to get to know him. He loves us, Karen—

he loves you—with an incredible love. Where is that kind of love in New Age thinking?"

Donna was surprised at her own words. She rarely felt comfortable talking about her faith with others. But it seemed something was tugging at Karen's heart. Yet when Donna looked at her, she couldn't read the expression on Karen's face. She didn't have a clue what Karen was thinking.

Blind choice:

Without looking ahead, turn to either page 107 or page 119.

"Uh, well," Donna stammered. "I think we should participate," she said finally. "If we do it right, I think we can use the Earth Day celebration as an opportunity to show New Agers Christians care about the world too."

"All right," Dennis shook his head. "It's done. We're in."

Dane and Bob congratulated Donna after the meeting.

"I think you made a good decision," said Bob. "Earth Day is a great opportunity to tell others about Christ."

"And to show the world we care," added Dane.

■

Earth Day brought booths and lectures and good wishes for the planet's future to the convention center. Between her shifts working in the CFTE booth, Donna walked the length of the convention center hall, picking up fliers and checking out exhibits. The recyclers' exhibit particularly impressed her.

Donna was fascinated by all she saw and learned. When she returned to check in for her second shift, Donna found Dane and Dennis praying with a college-age girl who had happened along and found something meaningful in what God had to offer.

Somehow Jesus had touched lives through Earth Day, just as he touched lives through other ordinary events in people's lives.

Donna left the convention center that evening filled with excitement about her Christian faith.

"We made a bold statement today," she told her mom later. "We told a whole city our creator is responsible for this world. And God cares about his creation."

"I'm proud of you, Donna." Her mom smiled. "It's a good feeling, isn't it?"

"The best!" Donna said. "The best."

The End

Over 100 children attended the party. Many of the parents stayed to help serve food and organize teams for the games.

Donna felt peaceful and happy as she stood back and looked at what was happening around her. Pin-the-Wings-on-the-Angel over in the corner. A treasure hunt for the older kids. A three-legged race on the shuffleboard court.

As they were cleaning up that night, Donna noticed Susan was unusually quiet.

"It was a huge success!" Donna assured her with a smile and a pat on the back. "Why so serious?"

When Susan looked up, Donna saw tears in her eyes.

"I can't believe how great it went!" Susan finally said. "I really didn't think it'd go this well."

"You had doubts?" Donna teased. "You?"

Donna and Susan shared a round of laughter as they headed into the kitchen. It had been the Lord's night after all.

The two girls promised each other the alternative party would be a community tradition from that night on. It would be a light for all to see—a light that brought glory to God.

The God of peace and love, Donna added silently.

The End

Confronting the problem just didn't seem like any kind of answer for Donna. What was so wrong with it all, anyway?

Donna turned back to the dessert table and scooped a slice of Mrs. Letterman's pecan pie onto her plate.

■

Donna waited all week for the Halloween block party. Karen had invited her to attend this once-a-year bash over on State Street. Everyone was coming in costume, and it was sure to be a real blast. Karen had helped Donna put together a gypsy costume, which she tucked inside her overnight bag underneath about five pounds of jewelry and a pair of satin shoes she'd found at the bottom of the bin at the thrift store.

Donna was putting the finishing touches on her makeup at Karen's when she heard the others arrive at the front door. Vampires, cowboys and goblins joined them as they headed off to the party, in full gear, on State Street.

Several of the houses were decorated as haunted houses with scary music and flickering candles. Donna had never seen so much Halloween enthusiasm in her life, and she munched from every table along the crowded street.

When most of the kids had eaten enough, someone suggested going back to Kurt's house and joining a game of Dungeons & Dragons already in progress.

"I don't know how to play," Donna confided in Karen.

"It's all right," she assured her friend. "Just watch. It's great fun."

■

Alan, the vampire, referenced a book called *The Masters' Guide to D&D* at the beginning of his turn. "I call upon the mighty emperor!" he spoke in a demanding tone. "Your assistance, oh, imperial one, Tramus, spirit of the battle."

Donna snatched up a copy of what appeared to be a game rule book and opened it randomly. "Another important attribute of the cleric," she read, "is the ability to turn away (or actually command into service) the undead and less powerful demons and devils."

Donna closed the book, set it back down and began to watch, amazed. Alan and the other players at the table were so

immersed in the game they seemed blissfully ignorant of their surroundings. Their eyes were open, but they were seeing another
world—an imaginary world so real to them Donna found herself
somewhat envious. She wanted to play too. She wanted to battle
with swords and spells and magic. It was exciting, and she knew
it could only be *more* exciting to be a part of it.

She continued to watch as the players acted out battles that
took place in their minds, as real as any battle Donna could imagine. They waged war against monsters and fought their way
through mazes and tunnels and dangers untold.

■

It was after midnight when Kurt's parents finally broke up
the game and sent the players on their way.

"What do you think of D&D?" Kurt asked Donna as they
were leaving the family room.

"I think I'd like to play sometime," she admitted. "But it's
pretty intense!"

"You're not kidding," Kurt bellowed, and he held out his
hand, a mass of stitches and flesh not quite healed, to Donna.
"We don't even know how this happened! We were all so into the
game."

"You don't know how it happened?" Donna asked. "If it's
that dangerous, why would you keep on playing?"

Blind choice:

*Without looking ahead, turn to page 54 or page 93 for Kurt's
answer.*

After several moments of silence, Donna answered her mother. "I want to go back," she said. "I've found something good there."

Donna could hardly wait for the next Sunday. At church that morning she witnessed the most amazing show of loyalty she'd ever seen. Two longtime members responded to Pastor Wyman's plea for financial assistance by signing over to the church their summer home and the land that it had been built on.

Pastor Wyman was near tears as he thanked them and then turned to the congregation.

"Isn't this the most incredible thing you've ever seen?" he began and then fell to his knees and lifted his hands toward the sky. "Oh, God!" he cried. "Oh, God! If only the rest of us could be so self-sacrificing, so giving, so like you, to renounce our worldly possessions, to turn our backs on the things of the world we hold dear. If only you would touch each one of us in this divine way!"

Many others came forward with jewelry and car keys and pledges of assets to be turned over to Pastor Wyman and the church. Donna could hardly believe her eyes as member after member came forward. The congregation went wild—cheering and crying, laughing and lifting their hands.

"This is what it's all about!" Susan said to Donna. "You don't see this kind of joy in other churches. We are so blessed here!"

■

"Incredible, wasn't it?" David asked as he approached Donna after the service had finally ended.

"I've never seen anything like it!" Donna told him.

"The sad thing is you probably never will anywhere else," Susan said, and she shook her head with regret.

"She's right," Kathy added. "I imagine it's all pretty overwhelming for a newcomer, huh?"

"Well, yes," Donna finally nodded.

"Listen," David suggested, "why don't you come on the weekend retreat?"

Donna had read about it in the church bulletin. Church members of all ages were encouraged to come for lectures, teaching and worship.

"That's a great idea!" Susan chimed in. "You can really get a feel for what we're all about."

Donna agreed, and she looked forward to it all week long.

She and Susan walked to and from school together every day, and their conversations centered around the church and Pastor Wyman.

■

By the time they arrived at Bennington Lodge, Donna was eager to learn whatever they had to teach her. Pastor Wyman even had planned a special session for children of divorce.

During the session, the leader matched up Donna with David as her partner. The instructor told them they were going to participate in an exercise to break down inhibitions. Standing with her back to David, Donna was to slowly let herself fall backward.

"The aim here," the instructor explained, "is for you to trust. No matter who may have let you down before, you're a new person now. This congregation is a family ordained by God, and Pastor Wyman is our father. You are brothers and sisters. And you must learn to trust each other, blindly, knowing you love each other and would never let each other down."

Donna trembled a bit at the thought. How did she know David would catch her? "Maryanne?" she spoke up. "I'm not so sure about this."

"No questions, Donna," the instructor interrupted. "Trust David. Trust this congregation. Trust!"

Donna apprehensively took her position and slowly fell backward. David did catch her after all, but she was still shaking several minutes later, although she couldn't say just why.

Donna could hardly wait for the positive-thinking lecture being held that afternoon. It was one of the most interesting offerings of the weekend.

"If God be for me, who can be against me ... If God be for me, who can be against me ..."

The class repeated that scripture aloud 10 times and then moved on to another.

"I can do anything through Christ who strengthens me ... I can do anything through Christ who strengthens me."

"Now close your eyes," the instructor told them. "Concentrate. Think about that problem, that trouble that has plagued you, that mountain you just can't seem to conquer. Picture it. Now, in your mind's eye, move that mountain out of your path! Talk to it! I can do all things through Christ! Tell it to move. Picture it moving out of your path. Set your sights on it! That's right."

Donna's eyes were closed so tightly they burned. "If God be for me, who can be against me?" she said aloud to the picture of her father in her mind. "Come home, Daddy. Come home. If God be for me, who can be against me?"

"Ask and you shall receive!" the instructor encouraged from the platform. "Seek and you shall find!"

"I'm asking," Donna told the vision of her dad. "Now I want to receive. Come back to us, in the name of Jesus Christ!"

Donna liked the power offered through positive thinking. She practiced it often throughout the rest of the retreat.

The leaders scheduled lectures and activities into every moment that weekend, and Donna couldn't find one spare minute to be alone. After dinner Saturday night, she opted for a quiet walk by the lake instead of the apple pie for dessert. She hadn't been out the door three seconds before Susan came up beside her.

"Going for a walk?" Susan asked. "Mind some company?"

"Actually," she began, "I had wanted to be ... "

"So, what do you think of the retreat?" Susan interrupted. "Pretty spectacular, isn't it? Pastor Wyman develops each and every one of these programs and chooses and trains the instructors himself. I always go home feeling so much more at peace, so much more in tune with my role in the church."

"What is that?" Donna inquired innocently.

"What's what?"

"Your role in the church."

Susan chuckled. "Our church is one body," Susan explained. "Each of us fits together with the others to make up the complete person." Susan paused. "You know, Donna, you really seem to fit with us here. Tomorrow we're having a special service where we admit new members. It'd be the perfect time for you to join the church."

Donna wondered if she was really ready to commit to Susan's church. Donna certainly felt loved there, but she kept remembering her mother's warning about the church's unusual practices.

What would you do?

If Donna joins the church, turn to page 79.
If she doesn't, turn to page 25.

"It's fun!" someone interrupted.

"Yeah," said someone else on the way out the door, "it keeps us thinking. On our toes."

"Exactly," Kurt finished. "It's not all-consuming. I was just careless that night. D&D stimulates the thought process. That's what my psychology teacher told us. That's where I learned to play, in class."

"It's so intense," Donna shook her head.

"So is football," Kurt smiled. "And I've been hurt a lot worse in a game of tackle in the back yard."

"I guess so."

"It's a great way to escape from the real world," Karen added as she joined them. "It's fantasy. That's all."

Donna didn't know what to think, which is why she accepted Tim's open invitation to the youth group to attend a seminar he had helped organize on the dangers of New Age beliefs. But Tim had misinformed her that the game Dungeons & Dragons would be discussed. Still, the seminar was interesting.

The speaker, Leland Craine, warned of a conspiracy. He told the audience that New Age and occult influences were becoming so commonplace that every person was at risk of attack.

Donna listened intently as Leland presented evidence of New Age beliefs in schools, in the military and even in corporate America through training seminars that emphasized visualization and the concept that you have the power within you to do anything.

Donna hadn't expected such a strong anti New Age message. Was Leland Craine on target? Or was he way off base? she wondered.

She listened carefully to the rest of his message.

What would you do?

If Donna accepts Leland Craine's perspective, turn to page 78.
If she rejects his perspective, turn to page 37.

Donna decided to stop listening to the tapes and using the meditation techniques until she could learn more. If they were going to lead her into the New Age stuff—or anywhere else away from God—she didn't want to take a chance on them.

"Tim," she said after class when the others had finally filtered out and headed off for church services, "I've been thinking."

"That's always nice to know," he teased.

Donna chuckled and then said seriously, "I couldn't stop thinking about what people were saying about meditation and the New Age movement. It scares me to think I might be getting into something dangerous. I mean, what if what Shari said is true? What if this stuff really does lead to other more dangerous things ... like Satanism or the occult? I'm going to stop using those techniques until I understand them better."

"If you really want to know more about what the New Age is all about and how it relates to your faith, you ought to come to a seminar I'm going to next weekend," he told her. "It's going to be held at my old church in Belwith Gardens. Would you like to be my guest?"

"Sure," Donna beamed. "I really do want to learn more."

■

Tim Benson and his wife Grace were right on time to pick up Donna. She'd overslept and nearly fell as she stumbled down the hall toward the front door.

"Careful, honey!" her mom called out.

"I'm okay, Mom," she called back. "See you tonight." And she was out the door.

As she opened the car door, she was surprised to see Bob sitting in the back seat.

"Bob?" Donna questioned. "What are you doing here?"

"Tim thought I might like this seminar too," he explained.

"Great!" Donna grinned. "This is going to be fun!"

The main speaker, Leland Craine, was a fairly handsome man with gray hair and a deep voice that made you want to listen, no matter what he was saying.

"Does it sound alarmist to you," Leland asked his attentive audience, "when I say there is a plot ... a conspiracy? An organized plan to destroy the Christian church, to blow away any and all traces of the family unit? Well, if I am called an alarmist, then so be it. Let me be the alarm! Let me sound the call to anyone who will listen!"

"The enemy has invaded our business world, our entertainment world through films, music, even television," Leland continued. "He has found a niche for himself in our schools and in our military. The enemy has entered every aspect of life. He is both subtle and blatant, and he has left no stone unturned."

Donna hadn't expected such a strong message. Was Leland Craine on target? Or was he way off base? she wondered.

She listened carefully to the rest of his message.

What would you do?

If Donna accepts Leland Craine's perspective, turn to page 78.
If she rejects his perspective, turn to page 37.

It was 9:45 p.m. Donna's mom was up and moving around the kitchen. Donna knew she'd never be able to sneak out until her mom settled down for the evening.

"You still up, honey?" Donna heard her call from the hallway.

"I'm getting into bed right now," she answered.

"Good night, then."

"Good night." Donna stood by the door, waiting, listening, until she heard the snap of the hall light going off and the scuff of her mom's old terry-cloth slippers making their way into the kitchen.

Donna slipped the serpent ring on her finger, pulled out the upside-down cross from where it was tucked inside her sweater and scurried to the window. A moment later, Donna was racing down the street.

It was after 10 when she finally arrived at Chaz's house. Through the window, she could see the flicker of candles.

She recognized Chaz, dressed all in black, through the window.

Chaz and three other guys were gathered around a board of some kind, their hands on a triangular game piece. Two girls were looking over their shoulders. The piece seemed to move around the board beneath their fingers, and their eyes all danced with a similar glow of anticipation. Donna walked inside without knocking and took her place behind Chaz without interrupting. She watched as the triangular piece moved across the Ouija board from letter to letter: A-L-L-I-S-T-E-R.

"The name of the spirit who will lead us tonight," Chaz told Donna. "Now that Donna's here, let's begin."

Donna followed the others' lead, her heart racing as they formed a circle around the three black candles Chaz was lighting. She quietly watched as the others in the circle closed their eyes. A surreal buzz of voices drifted around the room, and Chaz grasped her hand. Then everyone seemed to softly float into a trancelike state. Chaz's hand began to twitch in hers.

"Spirit of the night, we implore you," Chaz shouted, and Donna jumped in surprise. "Allister, spirit of the night, lead us this evening into your world."

Donna thought she could hear wind in her ears, and it seemed to lull her. Suddenly, Rhonda, one of the two girls across from her, began to groan in a guttural voice.

"It is I," she blurted in a voice very different from her own.

"Allister?" Chaz inquired.

"Yes," Rhonda said for Allister. "It pleases me you have called me out of the world of the dead."

"You honor us with your presence," answered Chaz. "How may we serve you?"

Donna was so engrossed in the spirit's speaking through Rhonda she almost missed what the spirit was saying. After describing his history, the spirit invited them to join him in the world of the dead. When they agreed, they were all instructed to close their eyes and take several slow, deep breaths.

What followed was an instant of travel—a rapid movement, so brief, yet so intense. Donna thought she was actually being lifted by some invisible force into another world. A free-fall dive into a black hole. She wanted to open her eyes, but she couldn't. She wanted to scream, but she couldn't do that either. Then, as suddenly as if she had been dropped, Donna felt herself caught up, and the power with which Donna felt herself catapulted back to the reality of Chaz's living room was more concentrated than anything she had ever experienced before. For the first time in her life, she was both exhilarated and terrified at precisely the same instant.

"What happened to us?" she asked Chaz the moment the meeting broke up. "What was that?"

"Incredible, wasn't it?" Chaz chuckled.

"Chaz, what was it? What happened?" Donna struggled to restrain her feelings of panic over what she'd been through.

"There's a world out there, Donna," he explained. "There's a natural, spiritual world out there available to anyone who wants to explore it. It's not something to be feared. It's like space, and we're the astronauts. It's an adventure, Donna. Another part of life that enriches us spiritually and physically. It's not to be missed."

What would you do?

If Donna gets more involved, turn to page 47.

If Donna pulls back, turn to page 109.

"Frankly," Pastor Hanley began, "I'm a little concerned about Bob. These tapes and books are filled with New Age philosophies."

"I thought so," Donna told him.

"I'm glad you brought this to my attention," the pastor said with a smile. "I'll have Tim talk to Bob about these tapes and books. You know, Donna, lots of Christians assume this New Age stuff is harmless. But I don't."

"I guess I have my doubts too since I came to you about Bob."

"Don't worry," he reassured her. "You did the right thing. You can help others discover the dangers of the New Age stuff— and the real truth in Jesus. You've got a lot of good insights."

"Thanks," said Donna. "Maybe I will."

Pastor Hanley's words came back to her a few days later when she went to Karen's house after school.

Karen's bedroom was littered with posters and cassette tapes that seemed to promote New Age philosophies. The books on her shelves focused on meditation, yoga, holistic therapy and the channeling of spirits.

I always thought Karen was a Christian, Donna thought. But maybe I've been wrong. These books seem so New Age. I wonder if I should say anything.

"Are you a New Ager?" Donna finally asked her.

"I don't like labels," Karen grinned. "I just get my meaning in life from lots of different sources. Why? Are you into this kind of stuff too?"

"No, I'm a Christian," she smiled.

"Oh boy, a Christian," Karen sighed.

"What does that mean?"

"Most Christians I've known criticize what I believe all the time."

"Well, our beliefs are different."

"Not really. I believe in a higher power the way you believe in God. I believe in Jesus—he was a great teacher. I worship many forms of your Jesus. Former prophets and teachers."

"You believe Jesus was just one of lots of teachers then?" Donna inquired.

"Yes."

"That's the part I don't understand about this New Age stuff," Donna said. "If you read about the life of Jesus, just the gospels without the rest of the Bible, you know Jesus was either the one and only way to God or else he was the biggest nut-case who ever lived."

Karen's eyes grew wide. "Donna ... "

"It's true," Donna assured her. "He said he was the only way to God, and I believe that. That's why what you and I believe is more than just a little different."

Karen didn't respond.

"Karen," Donna said, "do you have a Bible?"

"Yeah, sure." And she pulled it off one of the shelves where it was sandwiched between a book on astral travel and another on psychic healing.

"Look up John, chapter 14, verse 6," directed Donna.

Karen flipped through the front and then the back of the Bible looking for John. Finally, after checking the table of contents, she found John and the verse Donna asked her to find.

"Read it," said Donna.

"Jesus answered, 'I am the way and the truth and the life. No one comes to the Father except through me,' " Karen read.

"That's what it all comes down to," said Donna. "In another place, Paul says God will use the so-called foolish things of the world to put to shame everybody who *thinks* they are so wise and know it all. There's only one way to God. One way to happiness. One way to fulfillment. And, only one way to God's love. Karen, Jesus Christ is that way."

Time ticked away, and Karen didn't respond. Donna couldn't read the look on her face.

Blind choice:
Without looking ahead, turn to either page 107 or page 119.

"Okay, Mom," Donna smiled. "I'll give it a try." Donna would've rather told her mom no thanks, but she trusted her mom's advice. She'd try it once anyway.

■

Donna wondered why she hadn't heard about the Christian Concerns group before, but she was happy to discover a notice about it in the Sunday bulletin.

When she arrived at her first meeting, Donna noticed a lot of kids who didn't attend church or Sunday school were there.

"I've been into it all," Dane told the group from his place in the corner, his leg up on the desk beside him. "I tried the crystals and the potions and the heavy metal scenes. It's just not substantial. It's nothing to hold on to."

"But it's very persuasive," Donna found herself adding. "It's hard to turn away from. Besides, what's so non-Christian about visualization or caring for the environment?"

"I don't know about you," Dane began, "but I can't seem to get around that scripture that says, 'I am the Alpha and the Omega, the Beginning and the End.' For me, that says it all. Jesus is the only way to a full life."

After the meeting, Donna walked up to Dane. "Dane," she said. "Do you really feel the way you say you do? about God?"

"Yeah," he said nonchalantly. "I've tried almost everything to find a purpose in life. But I always seem to come home to Jesus. You know? I can't speak for anybody else. But I've found my answer."

"Dane, Donna," called Janelle. "We're going for pizza. Wanna come?"

Donna and Dane both nodded and then ran to catch up with the others.

Donna felt at home with this group, like she'd found the niche she'd been searching for. She suddenly felt close to God as she sat there in the restaurant surrounded by people her age who knew something about the things she'd been going through.

"I have this idea," Dane said between pizza bites. "What if we started some sort of outreach to kids our age? Kids who care about what's happening in the world, who might not know God's love."

"Yeah," Donna chimed in. "That's a great idea."

"Or we could join CFTE," Janelle offered. "It's a Christian environmental group I heard about—Christians for the Environment. They reach the kind of people we're talking about. We might get a chance to tell them about God's love."

"What's the environment got to do with anything?" asked Bob.

"I think I know," began Donna. "One of the things that really gets New Agers excited is caring for the environment."

"What would you like to see us do, Donna?" Dane asked from across the table. "We could start our own group or join CFTE."

An outreach group would be wonderful, she thought, but it's so easy to turn people off when telling them about Christ. Maybe the environmental group would be a more subtle way to live out their faith.

What would you do?

If Donna suggests they join the environmental group, turn to page 117.
If she suggests they organize an outreach group, turn to page 67.

"Will you stop it?" Donna shouted. "It won't work, do you hear me? I'm not gonna be swayed by your crying!"

"Donna, that's not what I ... "

"Just be quiet and leave me alone," she interrupted.

That night Donna decided it was time to make her move. She waited until Joe had been snoring at least half an hour and then carefully untied from her wrist the scarf that bound her to her mother. Donna didn't waste a moment—out of the tent, down the path, into the forest, across the stream and over to the highway heading west.

Donna was on her way "home."

With Pastor Wyman's help, Donna composed a letter to send to her mother. Donna wrote she was sorry her mom couldn't accept her new life but no one could change her mind.

Certain her mom would give up looking for her, Donna became more secure in the life she was making for herself. She devoted herself to Pastor Wyman's cause, and in time, Donna became the pastor's personal secretary.

One day she overheard a conversation between the pastor and his closest assistant, Susan's father, Arnold. They mentioned by name an elderly lady from a nearby town who'd become involved in the church, a lady Donna had come to like very much. She heard Pastor Wyman making a reference to her "deeds and bonds." Donna listened closely in surprise as the conversation uncovered things she didn't want to believe.

Evidently Pastor Wyman had been using all the money given to the church for his own purposes. And Susan's dad was in on the scam! While Pastor Wyman preached about poverty of spirit to his congregation, he was getting rich—very rich.

Donna was sickened by what she'd heard. How could I be so blind? she thought. That night Donna tucked as much as she could into a backpack and headed out of the community. She didn't know where she was going, but she knew she had to leave. She considered calling her mom, but dismissed the idea. She'd said goodbye to that life a long time ago. It was too late to turn back now. She'd make a new life for herself.

Isolated from her past, Donna headed down the road, looking for a kind motorist who could take her away. Anywhere. Alone.

The End

Pastor Hanley scratched his head and smiled at Donna.

"I think it's a mistake," he began, "to concentrate on the bad in things rather than on the good. Yes, there are some New Age principles in the material. But that doesn't make it all bad. In his first letter to the Corinthians, the Apostle Paul tells us the strange spiritual powers of unbelievers are nothing more than superstitions to us as Christians. We don't have to be afraid of them. Instead, we should learn what we can from New Agers and focus on that. It's not like the New Age stuff is a conspiracy out to end Christianity as we know it."

Donna listened intently but wasn't sure she agreed with her pastor's assessment of the New Age philosophies.

■

At the next Christian Concerns group meeting, Donna talked about her concerns with the group. She wondered if there wasn't more she could do to help kids who mistakenly think New Age thinking is compatible with Christianity.

"Somehow," she told them that night, "I know we can reach them. But we have to do it on their level."

"Why not look at their concerns, their beliefs," Tim suggested, "and approach them on some common ground?"

"New Agers are really into the environment," said Dane, a tough-looking guy who always sat in the back of the room. "We could join a Christian environmental group."

"Or we could organize our own outreach," someone else chimed in. "We could be bold about our concerns and help people understand the lies of New Age thinking."

"You brought up this issue, Donna," Tim added. "What do you think?"

An outreach group would be wonderful, she thought, but it's so easy to turn people off when telling them about Christ. Maybe the environmental group would provide a more subtle way to tell others about God's love.

What would you do?

If Donna suggests they join the environmental group, turn to page 117.

If she suggests they organize an outreach group, turn to page 67.

Suddenly the decision became easy for Donna to make. All she could think of was that defenseless little animal, hideously murdered before her very eyes.

Donna called Pastor Hanley the next morning and set up a meeting.

Donna felt her throat tighten as she told her mom and Pastor Hanley the whole story. She almost couldn't finish the story due to her coughing, wheezing and crying.

"Donna," was all her mother could say. "Oh, Donna."

"I'm so sorry," she said.

"I know someone who can help you," Pastor Hanley gently interjected as he pushed his glasses back up on his nose. "That is, if you want the help."

"She does!" Mom blurted a little too strongly and then looked into Donna's eyes as she turned around. "Don't you, honey?"

"Yes, Mom," she admitted. "I do." And the coughing began again, this time harder and more violent.

■

"It's so hard," Donna cried, wiping the tears from her eyes. "I want to break away, but they just keep calling and calling. They're wondering what's happened to me. Chaz has actually threatened my life if I try to leave the coven."

Donna heard her mother gasp from the corner where she was supposed to sit quietly for moral support.

"I sometimes want to go back," she admitted. "It's crazy, but I can't seem to help myself."

"Have you ever returned?" the counselor asked directly.

"You mean gone to any of the meetings?" Donna asked. "No, I haven't."

"You're becoming stronger, Donna," he assured her. "Hang in there, it will get easier."

Donna held onto that promise like a lifeline. In fact, it *was* her lifeline. It was all she had to hold onto in the world.

■

Donna thought the meeting that night would be a perfect opportunity to talk to the coven as a group. Maybe they'll understand. She remembered how supportive Chaz had always been before—before the séances, the drugs and the sex.

"I just need out," she told them matter-of-factly, only a slight hint of trembling in her voice. "Please understand."

After a long silence, Chaz spoke up. "It's not that simple, Donna. You don't just quit."

"Can't I be divorced?" she suggested hopefully. "Or excommunicated or something?"

"It doesn't work that way," said Rhonda smugly.

"Look," Donna toughened. "I'm leaving the coven. I'm out."

"I don't think so," Chaz replied.

Blind choice:

Without looking ahead, turn to page 15 or page 75.

"Karen?"

Karen was so deep in thought she hadn't even heard Donna say her name.

"Karen?" Donna repeated.

"Oh, sorry," she smiled. "I was thinking about what you said. The love thing, I mean. I haven't felt very loved as long as I can remember."

"Being loved by Jesus isn't like anything you'll ever experience," Donna beamed. "It's confidence, trust that no matter what you do or where you go, he's there with you."

"It takes a lot of faith, Donna," Karen said, "to turn your whole life over to someone you don't even know exists."

"He exists," Donna assured her friend.

"You seem so ... happy when you talk about Jesus," Karen smiled. After a long silence, Karen looked hard into Donna's eyes. "What do I do?"

"Well, ask Jesus to be the Lord of your life ... just ask," Donna said gently.

■

The changes Donna began to see in Karen encouraged her. One Sunday evening, Donna decided to talk about the experience with her youth group.

"I wish you could've been there!" Donna said. "It was so incredible to see Karen choose Jesus over the beliefs she'd had for so long. I wish we could do something to reach out to others like Karen—people who have fallen into stuff like New Age thinking."

"Maybe we could start our own outreach," said Bob. "We could start some kind of group to help other teenagers know what it means to be a Christian."

"Or we could just get involved in a group that's already doing something like that," suggested Dane. Dane was a tough-looking guy with black hair pulled back into a ponytail. "There's a group called CFTE we could connect with."

"Christians for the Environment," Tim interjected. "I've heard of it."

"What's the environment got to do with anything?" asked Bob.

"People like Karen often get into environmental causes—you know, 'Save the earth,' 'Don't deplete the rain forests,' 'Don't kill the whales,' " Tim told them. "And because most environmental groups aren't Christian, people often get led into New Age thinking when they join. The 'we can make a difference' philosophy is part of their motivation for getting involved. But remember, these groups don't think God is a necessary part of the equation."

"That's why a group like CFTE would be great," said Dane. "People would get into it because of the cause and find Jesus in the process. It's a great way to tell others about Christianity."

"What do you think, Donna?" asked Tim.

An outreach group would be wonderful, she thought, but it's so easy to turn people off when telling them about Christ. Maybe the environmental group would provide a more subtle way to tell others about God's love.

What would you do?

If Donna suggests they join the environmental group, turn to page 117.
If she suggests they organize an outreach group, turn to page 67.

▼

Donna carefully said her goodbyes to Chaz, lying about a newly imposed curfew she just had to make. She knew her mother didn't know she'd even been out, but she could hardly wait to make it back safely to confess. Shadows danced around every corner on the walk home, and street lights cast eerie beams of light toward Donna through hazy patches of darkness.

She began to run, faster than she thought she could. Her emotions were out of control, and she was near tears when she finally forced her key in the lock and flew through the front door and into her mom's bedroom.

"Mom?"

Her mother stirred a little and then drifted back to sleep.

"Mom!"

Her eyes opened and focused on Donna leaning over her.

"Donna?"

"Mom, can we talk?"

Donna's mother blinked the sleep from her eyes and raised herself up just in time to welcome her daughter into an unexpected embrace. Donna began to describe the night's eerie events. Her mom could hardly take it all in, but she listened quietly until Donna was through.

"I'm so scared," Donna admitted. "It was horrible. Like something out of one of those terrible horror movies."

"You've experienced a little piece of what your Christian faith has been protecting you from all these years," her mother explained.

Donna knew what her mom said was true. She took comfort in the safety of her mom's embrace, something she hadn't done in years.

"Donna," her mom whispered, "maybe we should ask God for strength and peace."

"Yes," Donna nodded. She felt the overwhelming need to ask God's forgiveness, to ask him to protect her and help her forget all she'd seen and experienced at Chaz's house. When she finished her prayer, Donna drifted off into a much-needed sleep.

■

Donna sat alone in the cafeteria, eating her lunch.

Looking around, Donna noticed Susan sitting at a table alone. Donna found herself walking toward her. Better to be seen with Susan than to be seen alone, she thought.

"Hi, Susan. Whatcha doin'?" asked Donna as she walked up to Susan.

Susan looked up at her from the large, half-completed poster she was making with different-color pens and glitter paint.

"Making posters," she answered, a little stunned Donna even spoke to her. Donna and Susan had been childhood friends but parted several years prior because of the bittersweet reality of school politics.

"I can see that," Donna chided as she casually slipped into a seat across from Susan. "What for?"

"I'm working with my church on an alternative party for Halloween," she explained, setting down the orange pen.

"Alternative party?"

"I don't believe in Halloween," Susan said. "I think it represents evil, and I ..."

"I agree with you!" Donna interrupted. "That's a great idea, an alternative party."

Susan was obviously surprised.

"We should do something like that at *my* church!"

"Well," Susan began, "if you really mean that, maybe you and I could work on it together. We could include your church, and it could be sort of a community thing."

Their enthusiasm quickly grew.

"I've been working on some of the local merchants," Susan continued, "and I have a few donations of food and drinks."

"I know Mr. Malody at the bakery over on Fifth Street," Donna added. "I'll bet I could get him to donate some cookies or cupcakes or something."

"That'd be great."

When the bell rang, Donna could hardly believe the whole lunch period had passed. She and Susan made arrangements to walk home together that day, and Donna agreed to go to Susan's house afterward to continue their discussion and make plans.

■

Over the next few days Donna and Susan spent so much time together the foundation of their old friendship returned. They laughed, talked and confided in each other like they hadn't done in years.

The night of the party they were both at the recreation center ahead of time, placing balloons, preparing the food tables and flinging streamers over the rafters.

"What if no one comes?" Donna wondered aloud. "We've worked so hard. What if nobody ..."

"Stop it!" Susan snapped. "Don't think like that. We *can't* think like that."

Blind choice:

Without looking ahead, turn to page 87 or page 123.

"Our efforts won't be wasted," Donna reminded Dane and
Bob before the first meeting. "If just one person discovers God's
love it'll be worth it."

But the two teenagers who did show up only heckled them
and cast doubt.

"We feel we have a responsibility to care for the world
around us," Dane told them. "It was given to us by a God who
loves and trusts us to ..."

"I knew it!" blasted Greg, one of the visitors. "I knew you'd
use this 'concern for the world' stuff to present your Bible baloney.
Just another sorry witnessing session for the unenlightened."

The meeting quickly turned into an argument. Nothing was
settled and no real resolution ever reached. The group ended the
meeting out of futility. They were tired of arguing.

After two more meetings like the first one, Donna wondered
why she'd ever thought an outreach group would work. Donna,
Dane and Bob were the only youth group members who'd
attended anyway, and they felt alone in the fight.

After only three meetings, the outreach group disbanded.

■

"We failed," Donna groaned to Tim.

"You didn't fail, Donna," he smiled.

"What would you call it?" Dane added.

"As Christians," the youth director explained, "we won't
always succeed in the literal sense. Sometimes we'll succeed
simply by having made the statement we set out to make."

"I don't get it," Bob winced.

"Perhaps you planted a seed in the people who *did* attend
the meetings. Maybe someday they'll remember what you said
and will turn to God."

"I still don't know ..." began Dane.

"You don't always have to *see* the change for there to be
one. Your victory is in continuing to remain a faithful witness."

"I've heard my mom say that," Donna remembered. "She says
that often the biggest victory of all is to remain standing."

"We're still standing," Bob added, and everyone laughed and
smiled at his profound statement.

"But we don't have to stand still," added Donna. "Let's brain-
storm new ways to reach out to others."

With a chorus of "all rights" and a generous supply of high

fives, they sealed the idea.

Donna smiled inside. She knew God would guide them no matter where they headed next.

She was right.

The End

"Scorpio," Tanya exclaimed, blowing back a wisp of black hair that had fallen into her eyes. "What's up for me this week?"

"Let's see," Donna said as she scanned the page. "You're about to come into some money, but it warns you here to be very careful about how you spend it."

"That must mean my babysitting job for the Hansens at the end of the week. I'll get $100 for two days and one night. Be careful how I spend it. H'm."

"Do you really plan things by your horoscope?" Carly asked.

"Oh yeah," Tanya gushed. "You should really chart your whole year and follow it. It's uncanny how accurate it can be. Look, here's mine."

Donna leaned in to get a better look at the sheet of paper Tanya pulled from her backpack. She unfolded an 11×17 sheet filled with colors and print.

"Can I see that?" Donna asked as she moved in a little closer. She scanned the entire sheet, skimming over the month-to-month instructions on love, finances and academics. "What's this?" she asked, pointing to a list of dates in a block at the lower corner.

"Those are my best days for love," Tanya replied. "If I meet someone on those dates, I always go for it. Otherwise, I don't. Today's a good day for making friends," she added pointing to another box in the far corner, and she smiled broadly at Donna. "My family is going to a seminar this weekend," she suggested excitedly. "One of the classes is on how to do your own chart. Would you like to come?"

◾

Donna anxiously awaited the weekend and her planned excursion with Tanya. The seminar was so much more than horoscopes—it featured meditation and yoga, it helped people to find their inner self and purpose in this life, and it taught about reincarnation and spirit guides. Donna could scarcely take it all in. There were alternatives and answers on every side, and Tanya's enthusiasm was somehow contagious.

Donna found something unique in Tanya. And she spent every afternoon during the following week at Tanya's house, sharing ideas and concepts and learning more about the spiritual awakening Tanya's mother was certain was dawning inside of Donna.

"Now is the time to embrace the truth," Mrs. Williams encouraged. "It's a new age, Donna. These are the best times of your life. Your spirit will soar in a way it's never been free to soar before!"

It all sounded so wonderful Donna could hardly contain her own enthusiasm. She wished she could share her revelations with her own mother the way Tanya could with hers. But she knew her mom wasn't ready to be "set free" just yet.

At first it was relatively easy for Donna to skip church and go to the Sunday meetings with Tanya and her family. But, as time went on, Donna's mom became more inquisitive about the church she was attending with the Williams family.

"What's the name of their church?" Mom finally asked outright one Sunday night as they were working together on a stew for dinner.

"The name? It doesn't exactly have a name."

"What kind of church doesn't have a name?" Mom laughed. "I'm sure it has a name."

"They're really into environmental stuff and reaching your potential as a person," Donna said. "It's not exactly a traditional church."

Donna's mom stopped what she was doing, set the knife on the pile of carrots and faced Donna. "What does that mean?"

"Well, it's not like Pastor Hanley's church or anything, Mom. It's more modern."

"Do they preach the gospel?"

"Well, yes. An enlightened gospel."

"Enlightened? Donna, just what kind of church is this you've been going to?" her mom demanded. "What's going on with you?"

What would you do?

If Donna gets angry and defensive, turn to page 32.
If she's open and honest about her feelings, turn to page 68.

Before she fell asleep that night, Donna sifted through the events of the evening. She'd heard the term "obsession" in association with D&D, but she wasn't convinced D&D was anything but harmless fun.

That was it. Harmless, creative fun, she thought. Some people go skiing every weekend, and others like to go fishing. Kurt and his friends like to play D&D.

It was suddenly easy for Donna to drift off to sleep.

■

"I have information to share tonight that may shock some of you," Leland Craine said into the microphone at the podium. "Yes, you may walk away from here tonight wondering which asylum I've escaped from." The audience laughed, breaking the tension into easy pieces. "But my prayer is that you will be open to what I have to share. That you will see what I see. That you will walk out of here informed and armed for battle."

Donna squirmed on the old folding chair and waited for Leland to continue. She hadn't been too keen on attending this meeting when Tim, her youth director, had suggested it. But going with Bob had made the prospect a little easier. And now Donna was intrigued—she wanted to hear what Leland Craine had to say.

"The New Age," he said with a sigh. "A new world order. Global peace. So enlightened. So peaceful. So dangerous!" Leland paused as if to dare people to challenge his statement. "Harmless teachings of past lives, ecological concern, self-awareness, therapy—these harmless teachings could, if left to run their course, overpower Christianity as we know it!"

Donna looked over at Bob, but his attention was focused intently on Leland at the podium. She looked hard at him, trying to read the expression on his face.

Donna hadn't expected such a strong message. Was Leland Craine on target? Or was he way off base? she wondered.

She listened carefully to the rest of his message.

What would you do?

If Donna accepts Leland Craine's perspective, turn to page 78.
If she rejects his perspective, turn to page 37.

"I think CFTE sounds good," she replied. "We could waste a lot of time getting organized if we try to start our own outreach. CFTE is already organized—and it kind of does what we've been talking about doing."

Donna's suggestion sparked a lively discussion filled with enthusiasm for getting involved with CFTE.

After minimal research, the group agreed to attend a meeting held by CFTE the following week.

When Donna and Bob arrived a few minutes late in front of the community building where the meeting was to be held, Dane was the only other member of their group there.

"Where is everyone?" Donna asked Dane at the door.

"I'm it," he grinned, and the three of them headed in together.

The members of CFTE were mostly college-age and older. Donna felt out of place at first. But it didn't take long before the group embraced the threesome, welcomed them and congratulated them for their like concerns and views.

"New Agers have the right idea in terms of peace on our planet and the importance of an ecological stand," Dennis said from his place at the front of the room. "But we have obvious differences in terms of creation and the way we live our daily lives. We give all the glory and honor to the God we know created us and our world—they don't. We have to consider carefully whether or not to become involved in the Earth Day celebration they're sponsoring."

"I think we have to get involved," someone said from the back. "If we don't, we might be missing a prime opportunity to do what we're here to do—tell others about God's love."

"Yes, but several of the major sponsors are openly New Age groups," Dennis responded. "Can we afford to align ourselves with those groups?"

"Can we afford not to?"

"All right," Dennis conceded. "Let's put it to a vote."

It went around the room. For. For. Against. For. Against. Against. Donna remained quiet in the far corner, not sure of her stand and unprepared to cast a vote. She was anxious to see how it turned out, though, because she could see both sides.

For. Against. Against. For.

Donna looked around the room. She had determined this

was a responsible group, and she wanted to be involved in their work.

    Against. For. For. Against.

    "Donna?" Dennis called.

    "Huh?"

    "Donna, your vote?"

    "Oh, I'm not voting. I abstain," she said.

    "Sorry, Donna. It's a tie—we need your deciding vote," said Dennis.

    Donna looked at Dane and Bob and back to Dennis.

What would you do?

If Donna votes to join the Earth Day celebration, turn to page 86.
If she votes not to join, turn to page 128.

Several moments of silence passed before Donna finally asked Karen what she was thinking.

"I don't want to hurt your feelings," Karen replied, "but I think your religiosity is pathetic. There's so much to experience in life, so many ways to grow. You're really missing out!"

"And I think you're missing out," Donna responded.

"If it works for you, fine," Karen patronized. "But please don't push it on me. I find it simplistic."

Those words hurt. Jesus had commissioned his disciples to "go into all the world and preach the good news to all creation," and Donna felt as if she had just failed miserably.

■

"And she called it simplistic," Donna complained to her friend Susan the next day on the walk home from school.

"That happens," Susan tried to encourage her. "Sometimes people just aren't ready to know the truth."

Donna knew Susan was right, but she had wanted so much for Karen to see things the way she saw them.

"You know," Susan suggested, "you might want to come visit my church sometime. Maybe you could find some answers on how to confront New Age beliefs in a biblical way."

Donna looked over at Susan and nodded absently.

Donna had always thought Susan looked a bit peculiar. Susan's skirts were just a tad too long, and she often wore those clean-yet-outdated ankle socks that she folded down into pristine cuffs just above her shoes. Donna hadn't even wanted to walk home with Susan that day, but she didn't seem to have a choice since their strides had brought them unavoidably together at the crosswalk.

"Would you like to come on Sunday?" Susan asked. "My pastor is a dynamic prophet and teacher."

Donna couldn't help thinking Susan sounded like a church commercial. "I already attend a church, but I might be able to visit. I'll give it some thought," Donna promised as they reached the edge of her yard. "I'll let you know."

I really should be more friendly toward Susan, she thought. After all, we used to be best friends.

Donna turned and called to Susan who was already half a block down the street.

"I'd love to go!" she yelled.

"Great!" Susan replied. "We'll pick you up Sunday morning at 8, okay?"

"Okay."

Blind choice:

Without looking ahead, turn to page 55 or page 64 to see how the visit to Susan's church turns out.

Donna felt loved and accepted at Susan's church, and she wanted to go back again. But some of what her mom said made sense. Was Susan's church out of balance? She paused for a moment to weigh the issues.

Pastor Wyman's influence reached from the bottom to the top of Susan's church. That did seem a little out of the ordinary. And that rule requiring kids to get their pastor's permission to socialize with other kids seemed a bit strange too. The more she thought about it, the more reasons Donna discovered to stay away from Susan's church.

"Maybe I'm not so sure about this. The congregation seems to worship Pastor Wyman instead of Jesus," said Donna.

"And that could become a dangerous situation," her mom added.

"If it isn't one already," Donna added. "I think I'll tell Susan I won't be going back there again."

The following week, when Donna and her mom went to the airport to pick up a visiting missionary, they passed a young girl about Donna's age witnessing to the passers-by in terminal B.

"The truth is within you. Do you search for truth?" the girl asked as she approached Donna and her mother.

"No, I've already found it," Donna said confidently as they continued on their way.

While Donna's mom waited at the gate, Donna retraced her steps back to the girl in the terminal.

"Did you come back to discover the truth?" the girl asked.

"No," smiled Donna, "to tell you about it. Have you ever heard about Jesus?"

The End

Donna's worst fears came true one hour later when the recreation center, prepared for over 100 kids, echoed with the voices of only six.

"So what's with this place?" shouted a young teenager dressed as a grotesque demonlike creature. "Where's the action?"

"I think it's pretty clear," Susan said as she approached him, "occult costumes are prohibited here."

"Looks like people are too," he sneered. "Besides, the rules were to come as something created by God. He made Satan. I'm Satan."

"Don't comment on that," Donna whispered to Susan from behind her.

"The mask will have to go," Susan held her ground.

"Why? So I won't scare any of the little kids who didn't come?"

Susan, exasperated, turned and headed straight into the kitchen. Donna almost didn't join her, but something told her Susan was suffering as badly as she was.

"It's a flop!" Susan exclaimed the moment Donna walked in. "A stupid flop. I can't believe it."

"I can't either."

"Maybe Satan really is in control of Halloween night," Susan groaned.

"Don't you believe that!" Pastor Hanley chimed from the doorway. Donna could hardly look at him.

"Hi, Pastor Hanley," Donna managed.

"Remember the scripture that says God turns all things to good?" Pastor Hanley asked.

"For those who love God and are called according to his purpose," Donna finished. It was one of her favorite verses—Romans 8:28.

"Well," the pastor continued, "you must trust that scripture even when things look bad."

"Walk by faith, not by sight, is that it?" Susan added.

"Exactly," Pastor Hanley smiled. "You did that when you planned this party, didn't you?"

"A lot of good it did us," Donna groaned.

Pastor Hanley pointed to the basketball court where the meager crowd stood at the food table. "There are half a dozen kids out there you can still minister to in some way. You've already given them an alternative to Halloween. You weren't wrong to plan this party. You can still make it a success."

Susan and Donna exchanged wondering, raised-eyebrow looks.

"Shall we?" Susan finally said.

"I think so," Donna concurred with a smile.

Pastor Hanley patted them both on the back as they passed through the doorway and went out into the recreation center.

"Quite a crowd," Donna said sarcastically.

"With six you get egg roll," Susan teased.

Two more children walked in the door with their parents.

"And with eight you get a party!" Donna added. She and Susan headed over to the table to greet the guests, among them a fine-looking young teenager, his demon mask removed.

"What happened to your costume?" Donna asked.

He pointed to the mask dangling over the side of the table behind them. "Now I'm a kid," he smiled at Donna. "God created kids too, right?"

"He sure did," Donna grinned back. "He also made hot chocolate. How about a cup?"

"Don't mind if I do," the guy smiled. Donna watched as he poured himself a cup.

He seemed so happy, so different from when Donna first saw him come in wearing the demon mask. Or had her perception changed? The guy could've left when he saw what a failure the party was. But instead, he stayed. He even seemed to enjoy it.

Maybe the party wasn't a failure after all.

The End

"I see I've given you something to think about," Pastor Hanley said, interrupting Donna's tidal wave of thought.

"Yes," she admitted. "I think you may be right about dabbling in the occult."

"Just remember God's love is sufficient to carry you through all your difficult times," Pastor Hanley continued. "Satan can't offer that kind of promise."

"I know what I have to do," Donna smiled at him. "Thank you, Pastor Hanley."

■

Donna turned her bedroom upside down, gathering everything she'd collected in her exploration of the occult. Each book, each piece of jewelry, each and every item she felt had any occult connection got piled in the center of her bed. Donna was anxious to get rid of it all.

She burned the books in the fireplace and smashed the jewelry with a hammer before wrapping it up and tossing it into the garbage can out back.

"Forgive me, Jesus," she whispered as she stood over it. "Help me never to be misled again."

■

On the way to school the next day, Donna ran into her old friend and neighbor, Susan. Although the two hadn't said more than six words to each other in almost as many years, Donna felt strangely open toward Susan as they walked the final blocks together. Before she knew it, she was telling Susan how she had burned the occult books and smashed the jewelry.

"That's great," Susan encouraged her. "I'm so glad you decided your faith in God is more important than that occult stuff."

"It wasn't even hard to do," she told her honestly.

"There are so many things this world offers that are just Satan's tools to turn our heads from God," said Susan.

"You sound like Pastor Hanley," Donna giggled.

"That's your pastor?"

"Yeah," she nodded. "I went to see him and he said the same thing you just did. About the dangers in the world around us."

"Take Halloween, for instance," Susan added. "Society teaches us that it's okay once a year to dress up like goblins and ghosts and to scare our friends. But celebrating Halloween is like celebrating everything that goes against our Christian faith."

"I never thought of it like that," Donna realized.

Susan continued. "Society offers it in such an appealing, seemingly harmless way that we don't even question what Halloween means."

"It's too bad the churches don't work together," Donna suggested. "Offering something else."

"Like an alternative to Halloween," Susan added, and the wheels were already turning like crazy in both girls' heads.

"Why couldn't we ... "

"Get *our* churches to do it!" Susan finished. "Yeah!"

"A party! Even a costume party."

"But no ghosts or goblins or witches."

"Or vampires!" Donna said.

■

The night of the party came quickly. Donna and Susan were still hanging the decorations only a half-hour before the party was to begin.

"What if nobody shows up?" Donna said suddenly.

"Don't even say that," said Susan.

But Donna knew Susan shared her concern. Would the party be a success or a disaster?

Blind choice:
Without looking ahead, turn to page 87 or page 123.

"Mom, I've found something here," Donna told her carefully. "It's changed my life. It's meaningful. I don't want to go back to what I had before. It just doesn't meet my needs."

"Donna, this doesn't even sound like you," Mom said. "What's happened to you?"

"I've awakened. I'm finally aware for the first time in my life. I've discovered something, and like a fire in the night, it's drawing me."

"Oh, Donna."

"If only you could experience what I've found, Mom." Donna found herself suddenly angry with her mom. "You're so narrow-minded!" She ran to her room and slammed the door.

Over the next few months, Donna and her mother drifted apart. Donna spent more and more time with Tanya and her family, learning about the healing power of crystals and the adventures to be found through channeling.

Donna most liked the positive-thinking concepts and found comfort in diving into intense meditation and visualization. Her own life seemed so drab and unexciting—she liked the escape of visualizing a better set of circumstances.

Donna knew she didn't have all the answers. But her new beliefs promised she would—eventually.

Occasionally, Donna felt lost or depressed. And a few times she wished she'd explored Christianity further before choosing the enlightened path of the New Age movement. But Donna stubbornly stuck with her mixed bag of beliefs. Though she often felt unfulfilled or empty, she'd convinced herself things would improve.

Maybe my next life will be better, she thought.

The End

"Well," Donna started timidly, "I think that, uh, if we participate in Earth Day, we'll be compromising what we believe."

"Right!" someone shouted. "I'm with her!"

"Right!" another one agreed.

■

On the walk home from school the following Friday, Donna heard someone call her name.

"Donna! Donna, wait!"

Donna turned around to see her neighbor, Susan, running after her.

"Donna, I saw you at the CFTE meeting," she said. "You were great!"

"You were there?"

"Yeah," she told her as they walked on, "and I voted the way you did. I just wanted you to know that."

"Thanks."

"You know, Donna," Susan began, "my pastor believes the way you believe. He's very strong about it too, like you. Maybe you'd like to come visit my church Sunday."

Donna hadn't done anything with Susan in years. They'd drifted apart somehow. They obviously had something in common, and Donna thought she might like to visit Susan's church.

"Sure," she nodded. "That sounds like fun."

Blind choice:
Without looking ahead, turn to page 55 or page 64.

Donna winced a little as she headed toward her mom and Pastor Hanley. They looked a bit like a lynch mob.

"Where have you been?" her mom started.

Instead of answering, Donna glared at the pile of her things accumulated on the kitchen table. "You went through my stuff!" she roared. "How dare you do that! Don't I have any rights around here?"

"None I can think of," her mother said sarcastically. "Now start talking, Donna."

"You are not my master," she snapped.

Without another word, Donna ran down the hall. Her mother and Pastor Hanley followed close behind, but not close enough to reach her bedroom door before she slammed it shut and locked it.

"Donna! Open this door!" Her mother must have pounded on the door for 10 minutes before finally slinking away down the hall.

"Give her some time," Donna heard the pastor suggest, and she laughed at his gullibility.

"Yes!" she mocked them through the locked door. "Give her some time!" Donna sat down on the floor, a fat black candle lit in front of her, and closed her eyes. "Time to get loaded," she continued in a whisper. With that, Donna took a deep snort of cocaine her mom hadn't discovered. "I can deal with you two better when I'm loaded," she giggled.

■

Over the following months, Donna's drug use increased. She began experimenting with new drugs, mostly ones Chaz provided prior to the parties he hosted. They weren't the kind of parties most of Donna's school friends attended where people danced and ate pizza and maybe made out for a little while. Chaz's parties were wild, crazy parties where everyone had sex with everyone else and consumed thousands of dollars in drugs. Sometimes the parties were held at Chaz's and sometimes in the woods nearby—usually at the time of a full moon.

Donna's life revolved around those parties and around the rituals in the woods that had become more and more frequent. Chaz and the other coven members had tired of sacrificing dogs and cats and the like and had even begun talking about sacrificing a human being, perhaps a baby. The more innocent the better. It wasn't murder or anything, after all, when it was done in the name of religion. And that's what Satanism was—Donna's new religion.

Blind choice:
Without looking ahead, turn to page 14 or page 60.

Other

books available now:

He Gave Her Roses	(Sex and Dating)
Fast Forward	(Movies, Music and Television)
Just This Once	(Drugs and Drinking)
Looking for Class	(School, Careers and Success)
Not in My Family	(Family Problems)
The Option Play	(Sports and Competition)
A Time to Belong	(Friendships and Peer Pressure)

You'll meet Christian teenagers as they encounter decisions regarding these everyday, contemporary issues. Decide what you would do and learn the consequences. Each book has several endings and dozens of story possibilities. $6.95 each.

He Gave Her Roses
0-931529-92-1

Fast Forward
1-55945-048-7

Just This Once
1-55945-106-8

A Time to Belong
1-55945-051-7

Looking for Class
1-55945-061-4

Not in My Family
1-55945-022-3

The Option Play
1-55945-050-9